A History of the

EASTBOURNE AVIATION

COMPANY

1911–1924

by

Lou McMahon

and

Michael Partridge

Published by the
Eastbourne Local History Society
2000

ISBN 0 9504560 8 X

Typeset by John Surtees and Michael Partridge

Printed by Sumfield & Day Limited, Eastbourne

Published by the Eastbourne Local History Society
Website: www.sales@eastbourne-web.co.uk

Foreword

By Wing Commander R. P. Beamont

CBE, DSO*, DFC*, DL, FRAeS

One day in June 1944 when flying my Hawker Tempest at 400 mph over the Channel under radar direction in pursuit of a V1 flying bomb heading for London, I saw it briefly before it flew into the clouds ahead. It soon reappeared in a gap and I could see the front at Eastbourne and then dead ahead Eastbourne College (where I had been a new boy in '34). I had to attack the V1 before it got away to London (only about 10 minutes from the coast), but there was a clear risk to the town so I held fire briefly before shooting it down north of Polegate.

I had no idea that this action had happened over an area of important aviation history!

In the 1930s, during a 'Corps' day of rifle-shooting at the Crumbles range, someone said that there had been an aerodrome there once, but that was all I ever heard about it.

In their book the authors have brought together the factual history of Eastbourne's part in the beginnings of aviation, and have identified the pioneering personalities involved. F. B. Fowler who, in teaching himself to fly in 1911, became one of the founders of British aviation and went on to establish a flying school, to design and build his own aircraft, to develop a successful RNAS base and aircraft factory, and in the process train some very distinguished Naval and RFC pilots.

There is a fascinating account of the pioneering interception by R. J. Bone of one of the first German raiders which he pursued out to sea and forced down off Zeebrugge in 1916. Eastbourne-trained Bone flew from a field near Westgate which by World War II had become RAF Manston, the base of 609 Squadron's successful campaign against the notorious 'Tip and Run' raiders in 1942. A case of history repeating itself – and the C.O., one R. P. Beamont, was an Old Eastbournian!

This well-researched history is a worthy tribute to the part played by Eastbourne in the very beginnings of aviation.

Roland Beamont

September 1999

2. Frederick Bernard Fowler in 1912.

Contents

List of Illustrations

Our thanks for permission to reproduce photographs or drawings are due as follows:

The Aeroplane 65
Authors 39, 43, 103–105
Wing Commander R. P. Beamont, CBE, DSO*, DFC*, DL, FRAeS 1
The British Motor Industry Heritage Trust 3
Ian Burns 69
Mrs Mary Cooper 22, 74–89
The late Trevor Dowsett 60, 61
Bob Elliston 92
Flight International (for *Flight* magazine) 5, 9, 24, 25, 28, 35, 56, 63, 108–110,
112–120, 125
Wallace James Ford 12, 14, 17, 21, 64, 95, 97, 102, 124
Michael Goodall 4, 8, 22, 72, 74–89, 93
Ken Hart 70
Roger T. Jackson 42, 49, 99, 101, 123
Group Captain G. F. Lerwill, DFC 47
Stuart Leslie and Jack Bruce 10, 26, 55, 67, 68, 90, 111, 121, 122
Mrs Benita Moxon 16
The Old Wellingtonian Society 58
Tim Partridge 11, 20, 46
The Royal Aeronautical Society 27, 29
The RAF Museum 7, 13, 23, 36–38, 40–41, 44, 48, 51–54, 57, 59, 72
Lawrence Stevens 50
Sussex County Herald 98
The Towner Art Gallery and Museum 2, 6, 8, 15, 18, 19, 26, 30–34, 45, 62, 66, 71, 90,
91, 94, 96, 100, 111
Miss Eva Travers 73
Mr D. J. Vine and Mr and Mrs Gary Russell 22, 74–89

We apologise if we have accidentally omitted to acknowledge the use of any photographs
or drawings.

Introduction

The origins of this book go back some twenty years. In 1986, Eastbourne's Towner Art Gallery and Museum mounted an exhibition relating to the town's airfield and its brief life. The exhibition relied on material researched in the 1970s by Michael H. Goodall, an aviation historian, and on material collected by the late Gerald Newson, a freelance journalist, who was also researching the history of the Eastbourne Aviation Company. Indeed, he and Goodall collaborated to some extent. Goodall published his findings in *Air Pictorial* in March 1979; Newson had also written an article but was unable to find a publisher for it. In 1982 he sold his manuscript, together with a quantity of related material, to the Towner Art Gallery for £400. Some time afterwards the Eastbourne Local History Society agreed with Dr Patricia Andrews, then the Curator of the Towner, that the story was of sufficient historical interest to warrant publication. The material was not at that time in publishable form and it was agreed that Lou McMahon and Michael Partridge would undertake the task of consolidating the information on behalf of the Society.

Newson's manuscript had a tendency to ramble and his chronological sequencing was, not to put too fine a point on it, erratic. Frequently his research would take him down obscure and irrelevant trails, and he was also careless about citing his references and sources.

The task of authorship was demanding and, perhaps inevitably, the verification of sources opened up new research directions and these have been pursued diligently. We felt that, apart from the major players in the tale, the narrative lacked the substance and excitement that the personalities who embarked on the adventure of flying in 1912 would give to it. So it is without apology that the final text includes details of the lives and flying careers of the first 19 men who learned to fly at the St Anthony's airfield in Eastbourne as pupils of Frederick Bernard Fowler's flying school. We also became aware of the extent to which the airfield became, for a few short years, an inherent part of the life of the town. For years after its demise, townspeople continued to treasure memories of it in its heyday, not least because so many Eastbournians worked at the airfield or at the Seaplane Base, or had relatives who did.

We have also endeavoured to uncover some evidence about the period when the airfield became an RNAS Flying School and we have honoured those men who lost their lives during this time.

Thanks to the generosity of a number of individuals, it has proved possible to locate several photographs of the airfield and of the Seaplane Base, of the men and women who worked there, of the nineteen original airmen, as well as a collection of pictures of the aircraft in which they flew. Many of these have been incorporated into the text.

A final word of warning. This tale is as complete and as accurate as conscientious research is able to make it. More evidence will be uncovered as time passes and the authors would be delighted to receive comments and information which could be incorporated into a later edition. Inevitably we have used secondary sources on occasion and in some cases our sources remain unreferenced. A lot has been published about the Eastbourne Airfield that is of questionable accuracy. As is often the case, errors of fact in one publication are replicated in others. We hope that we have gone some way towards producing a record that is interesting, both to local residents and to aviation historians, that is tolerably accurate and which will serve later researchers as a reliable starting point.

The authors may be contacted on (01323) 638176 or (01323) 638914 or by e-mail at: partridge8@hotmail.com

Acknowledgements

We acknowledge with thanks the help provided by:

Members of the Eastbourne Local History Society: John Cant; John Surtees, for his help with word-processing of the text; Kevin Ward, for his painstaking research into the archives of the RAF Museum, which saved us many a trip to Hendon; Gounil Brown for her talented work on the cover painting; David Jeffery for drafting the plan of the Seaplane Base; and also Vera Hodsoll, Lawrence and Pat Stevens, Bob Elliston, Lionel Jones, John Claremont, Paul Fulford, Philip Brown and Stella Hardwick.

Mrs Mary Cooper of Thornton-Cleveleys, Wallace James Ford, Mr and Mrs Gary Russell, Mr D. J. Vine, Ken Hart, Stuart Leslie and Jack Bruce, Roger T. Jackson, Ian Burns and Ralph Barker for allowing us to reproduce photographs from their collections.

Michael H. Goodall for the generous loan of his files on the EAC; Miss D. Hillier, Librarian, Royal Military Academy, Sandhurst; John Sworder, Secretary, The Old Wellingtonian Society; E. Bruce Williams, The Old Bradfieldian Society; Brian Harral, for information about the life of F. F. Minchin; Trinity House Lighthouse Service; the Department of Research and Information Services, the Royal Air Force Museum, Hendon; M. D. Henderson of the Fleet Air Arm Museum, Yeovilton; the Department of Printed Books, the Imperial War Museum; the staff of the Public Record Office, Kew; the librarians of the Royal Aeronautical Society; Mike Fish of British Aerospace Archives, Filton; Fred Huntley, MBE, of British Airways Archives, Heathrow; Mike Marshall of the Croydon Airport Society; the Commonwealth War Graves Commission; Julian C. Temple of the Brooklands Museum Trust; Stephen Laing of the British Motor Industry Heritage Trust; Nigel Day of Sumfield & Day Ltd, printers, for his expert help in getting the typescript and illustrations into print; David J. Barnes, for access to his records of WW1 airmen; Paul S. Leaman, Managing Editor, *Cross and Cockade International*, for kindly consenting to proof-read the manuscript and for much helpful advice; Mr C. V. McCann, MBE, for allowing us unlimited access to his collection of *Cross and Cockade* journals; Stuart Leslie for kindly sharing, with generous good nature, some of his vast store of knowledge with us;

Hazel Lintott for her help in researching and then drafting the map at Appendix 1; Lorna Kenward, Eastbourne Central Library; Gordon Clark, of Eastbourne, for his helpful comments on an early draft of this text; Archie Jackson; Jo Honeysett; Peter Langridge; Roy Brooks; Alan Brown; Olive Samuel; Patrick Davis; Robert Armstrong; Mr T. Biron of Five Ashes; Christchurch Library; The Red House Museum, Christchurch; the late Trevor Dowsett; Nicky Ingram, former Local History Assistant at the Towner Art Gallery; the late Leslie Tapp of Westham; and many others who have responded helpfully to our letters and telephone calls.

Finally, we would like to record our thanks to wives, Pam and Sheila, for their unfailing support and forbearance.

All errors and omissions remain the responsibility of the authors.

Early Days

There can be no doubt that Eastbourne justifiably commands a place in early aviation history. Equally, there can be no doubt that much of the credit for that distinction belongs to Frederick Bernard Fowler, AFC[1], whose industry and foresight, so typical of aviation pioneers, led to the founding of the Eastbourne Aviation Company (EAC) on 1 December 1911.

The subject of aviation, however, had been discussed in Eastbourne before that date. On Sunday 25 July 1909, Louis Blériot accomplished the first cross-channel aircraft flight, landing at Dover, where a modest memorial not far from the castle marks his achievement. Nine days later, on Tuesday 3 August, his aircraft was on display in Eastbourne, as advertised in the *Eastbourne Chronicle* of 31 July 1909, an example of enterprise by Mr E. A. Brown, manager of the then privately owned Devonshire Park and Baths Company.

Earlier in 1909 letters had been received from the Secretarie-General of the Aero Club International requesting the assistance of the Corporation in establishing an Aerial Station in Eastbourne. A Special Committee[2] made up of members of the Pleasure Grounds and the Highways and Drainage Committees met on 25 February 1909 to consider the request. After much deliberation the Committee felt that the aeroplane industry was not yet sufficiently advanced to justify them in recommending to the Council to take any steps in the matter; also that it was a matter for private enterprise rather than for the municipality; but, assuming anything came from the suggestion, they thought a suitable site for the proposed depot could be found on the Crumbles. It was agreed that a copy of the minutes of the Committee Meeting be sent to local landowners; that any residents interested in the matter be invited to contact the Town Clerk; and that the Secretarie-General of the Aero Club International be requested to give further information as to the practicability of the scheme and to provide particulars of club members who flew aeroplanes.

Subsequently a copy of a letter from the Secretarie-General of the Aero Club International was sent by the Town Clerk, Mr H. W. Fovargue, to the Editor of the *Eastbourne Gazette* with a covering letter requesting that it be published in the paper and suggesting that any interested persons contact him with a view to being invited to a meeting of the Special Committee to consider the matter further. Both letters were published on 10 March 1909.

At Council Meetings on 9 September and 4 October 1909 it was resolved to establish an Aviation Committee[3] made up of Council Members and co-opted gentlemen to consider the possibility of making Eastbourne an aviation centre.

The Aviation Committee met on 14 October 1909 and considered letters from aeroplane constructors and the question of a site. It was resolved that the Aero Club be invited to send delegates to inspect three possible sites and advise on their suitability.

Hereafter the subject of aviation on the Crumbles fades from the Council minutes and private enterprise began along the road that was to lead to Frederick Bernard Fowler forming the Eastbourne Aviation Company.

Whether Fowler saw Blériot's plane at the time is not known, but in 1958, at the age of 75, in an article in a newspaper, the *Christchurch Times*[4], Fowler stated that it was Blériot's flight which aroused his interest in aviation. His enthusiasm was spurred by the feat to such an extent that within little more than two years Eastbourne had its own airfield followed two years after that by a seaplane base and a manufacturing facility.

Frederick Bernard Fowler

Fowler's family came from Woburn in Bedfordshire, where his great-great grandparents and possibly also his great-grandparents were engaged in the brewing industry. Sometime in the mid-19th century the business was sold and five brothers, of whom Fowler's father was one, shared the proceeds and went their separate ways.

Fowler's father moved to Sussex, where he became a farm bailiff on the Gage Estate, living at Tilton Farm, Selmeston, near Lewes. There on 11 June 1883 Frederick Bernard Fowler was born, the son of John Charles Fowler and his wife Margaret Elizabeth. These details are contained in entry number 652, dated 27 July 1883, in the baptismal register of St Peter's Church, Firle, which is in the adjoining parish.

Between 1905 and 1919 Fowler's father is shown in Eastbourne directories as residing at Avalona, a pleasant house at 57 Watts Lane. In Fowler's Certificate of Marriage, his father is described as 'gentleman'.

Michael Goodall, together with the late Wing Commander A. G. Loton, AFC, who features later in this story and who knew Fowler well from 1918 until his death in 1967, provided some of the following information.

After leaving New College[5], in those days one of Eastbourne's leading private schools, Fowler was apprenticed for five years (1901–05) with Vickers Sons & Maxim Ltd (now Vickers plc) at Erith, Kent, where he became a skilled turner and fitter and took a keen interest in internal combustion engines. He worked on, and on occasions drove the 20 hp Thornycroft[6] car in Tourist Trophy (TT) trials. He moved to the Climax Motor Company Ltd (later Coventry Climax) in Coventry as a foreman in 1905, returning to Eastbourne in 1907[7].

3. The 1904 Thornycroft 20 hp Tourer.

Ministry of Defence (RAF) Records[7] show that he served with the rank of Corporal with the 3rd City of London Yeomanry, a Territorial Unit, between 1902 and 1906.

Mr O. C. Morison

Eastbourne residents were forcibly reminded of the new science of aviation when, on 15 April 1911, a Blériot monoplane with a 50 hp Gnome engine crash-landed in Devonshire Park. The *Eastbourne Gazette* of 19 April 1911 carried a three-column article with photographs of the pilot, Mr O. C. Morison, and of his wrecked aeroplane, parts of which were suspended from a tree in the park. He had been flying from Shoreham to Eastbourne and was attempting to land in the park when, in trying to avoid some telephone wires, he struck a lamp standard which he had failed to see. Morison was well known for his dare-devil flying and was named by Dallas Brett[8] as one of the five leading pilots of 1911. He visited Eastbourne again in July when he landed in a Morane monoplane on the marshes to the rear of the Motor 'Bus Works at Roselands, asking a Mr William Townsend, who was the first to reach the spot: 'Is this Hastings?' He stated that he had started from Paris that morning and was afraid that his petrol might give out. His tank was refilled and he then took off and continued his journey to Brighton[9].

McArdle and Drexel

Late in 1911 Fowler met William E. McArdle, of McArdle & Drexel, whose New Forest Aviation School at East Boldre, Beaulieu in Hampshire, complete with eight aircraft, was being wound up. Despite parental doubts, but possibly with their financial assistance, Fowler purchased five of the aeroplanes: a two-seater and a single-seater Blériot, both with 50 hp Gnome engines, and three Blériot types with 25 hp Anzani engines. At this time Fowler had no airfield in Eastbourne, nor had he yet learned to fly. So it was agreed that he could store the aircraft at Beaulieu until he could move them to Eastbourne. It has often been stated that Fowler taught himself to fly at East Boldre and this is confirmed by his recollection in the *Christchurch Times* article of 1958. 'At first', he said, 'I tried to operate the machine on the ground, keeping to a straight line, and after getting the feel of the controls I ventured up to between 30 and 40 ft, still keeping in a straight line. When I eventually got the hang of the controls, I then did a circuit. I didn't smash a thing, but it was more luck than anything else.'

Fowler's Airfield

Fowler soon found his first site, some 50 acres of marshy ground between the gas works and St Anthony's Hill. This was rented from Mr C. F. Russell of East Dean who had the land on lease from the Duke of Devonshire. A clause was inserted in the lease to the effect that 'Should any farm animals be injured or killed by the 'planes, compensation was to be met by the Eastbourne Aviation Company'. Maps of the airfield (see Appendix 1) show that it was crossed by many open ditches (sometimes known as sewers or dykes) and this problem was overcome by boarding over the ditches, as can be seen in the photograph illustrated on the next page. By this means a runway of 580 yards (530m) was provided, quite ample for aircraft of those days.

4. Bernard Fowler and his airfield in 1912, showing the dykes and boards.

Fowler's Crash in the Solent

On 8 January 1912 (a week before he obtained his Certificate as a pilot), Fowler tried to fly one of the aircraft, a 50 hp Blériot, from Beaulieu to Eastbourne. In an interview[10], reported in an article in the *RAF Flying Review* in 1959, Fowler is quoted as saying:

'I left Beaulieu at about ten o'clock with good visibility over the aerodrome and practically no wind, but, on approaching Calshot, I ran into fog and in a matter of seconds was enveloped. My one idea was to get out of the fog and I started to turn but, without any horizon to guide me, I soon lost control and actually flew into the water about the middle of the Solent [between Calshot and Cowes]. An air bag in the fuselage probably saved my life, as the machine did not sink at once and I managed to rid myself of most of my heavy clothing before the aircraft disappeared. The Gunners[11] who then occupied Calshot Castle heard the crash and eventually found me just as I had given up all hope. At Calshot I was treated with the greatest kindness, given some dry clothes, hot drink, and after I had recovered I was taken to Southampton in their launch.'

Fowler must have felt some embarrassment over his ditching in the Solent, for later, in January, he was moved to write to the editor of *Flight*[12] as follows:

'As there were many and varied causes assigned for my accident in the daily papers, I should be pleased if the true reason appeared in your paper. The facts of the case were this: as soon as I got over Southampton Water I ran into a thick bank of fog, blown up by the wind which had freshened considerably. I could hardly see 50 yards ahead, and rather than run the risk of getting lost I decided to turn and get back to land. In the turn I must have dropped considerably, and owing to the fog, before I had time to realise it, I found myself uncomfortably near the water. I did all I could do to get the machine to rise, but owing to there being a stiff breeze behind me I could not get her up quick enough, with the result that I struck the water going all out. Needless to say she turned a somersault and smashed herself almost to atoms. The air bag I had on kept her afloat, although even with that the only part that I did keep above water was the tail and elevator.'

The remains of the aircraft were later towed ashore.

The EAC Trailer

The other machines were transported from Beaulieu to Eastbourne by road on a trailer specially constructed at the aerodrome for the purpose. This trailer was illustrated in a short article in *Flight* magazine on 6 January 1912. It was described as consisting of the front and back wheels of an ancient Oldsmobile, fixed to an ash frame made from 3 by 2 inch timber. The undercarriage of the machine was firmly bolted to this framing and the wings carried in a felt-lined trough fixed on either side.

5. The EAC Trailer.

The journey of 110 miles was accomplished at an average speed of 15 mph. Despite the total length of the car and trailer being about 43 ft, no difficulty was experienced, even in negotiating right-angle corners.

Fowler's Certificate

On Tuesday 16 January 1912, Fowler was awarded RAeC Certificate[13] No 175. *Flight* of 6 January 1912 gives details of his test flight: 'Making his test for the Royal Aero Club Certificate, Mr F. B. Fowler, at Eastbourne on December 27, made five figure eights during 17 minutes at an average height of 200 ft, and then landed within two yards of the centre of a circle of 200 yards. The machine was a 50 hp Gnome-Blériot'.

6. F. B. Fowler with his Blériot.

Major General T. H. F. Foulkes, CBE, OBE, whose aunt was Fowler's first wife, recalled, in a conversation with Gerald Newson, 'I remember Fowler well in 1917 or 1918 when I was ten. In our family he was admired as an intrepid aviator and early motorist. It was said that he had many escapes from death in the air and on the road'.

Victor Yates

While Fowler had been negotiating the purchase of the five aircraft from McArdle & Drexel, another would-be aviator was busy constructing an aeroplane at Wilmington, six miles north-west of Eastbourne. He was Victor Yates, who in 1911 had a motor and motorcycle business at 62 Cavendish Place in Eastbourne, adjacent to the Fire Station. By 1912 local directories show him as having moved to 61a Cavendish Place. In 1911 Yates designed and built an all-metal monoplane, powered by a 35 hp Alveston engine. The aircraft was constructed from steel tubes and fittings in a tarpaulin-covered wooden structure in a field owned by a Mr Gribble of Milton Street. Yates's aircraft was clearly remembered by Mr H. J. Paine of Wish Hill, Willingdon, and Mr A. E. R. Marsh of Broad Road, who worked at the EAC as a fitter and turner from 1913 to 1917 and 1919 to 1921, in letters written to Michael Goodall in 1973.

7. Victor Yates in 1912.

The *Eastbourne Gazette* of 5 July 1911 carried a photograph and extensive description of the aircraft. The machine was 25 ft in length with a wingspan of 34 ft. It was controlled 'by one steering wheel which can direct the steering rudder and the rear wheel by one movement; another movement sets in motion the elevation which causes the machine to rise or fall; a third works the ailerons which operate the wings and regulate the proper balancing of the aeroplane. There are two seats, one for the driver and the other for the passenger'. As well as the fuselage, steel tubing was used for the framework of the wings, which were covered with canvas, laced through the tubes and pulled tight. The aircraft had three landing wheels, each 24 inches in diameter with 3 inch tyres. By the time the aircraft was completed, the grass had grown so high that take-off was impossible; indeed Mr Trevor Dowsett recalled that Yates was told by the farmer to 'get that thing off my field'. The *Eastbourne Gazette* of 26 July 1911 carried a report that flights of Mr Yates's new aeroplane had been postponed for lack of a suitable landing space. He was stated to be

8. Victor Yates with a 50 hp Blériot.

willing to pay a fair rental and give a guarantee against injury to cattle. Perhaps it was this notice that came to be seen by Fowler, for it was reported that Yates's aircraft was moved to St Anthony's Hill, though there are no reports of it flying.

Thereafter Yates seems to have joined forces with Fowler at St Anthony's. Certainly Yates's business does not appear in *Gowland's Eastbourne Directory* after 1912, though he was living at 8 St Anthony's Avenue, near the airfield entrance, in 1913. We also have evidence from Mr S. N. Wenham that both Fowler and Yates lodged with his parents at 16 St Anthony's Avenue, though whether before or after this date is not clear.

In February 1912 Yates took off from the airfield in a 50 hp Blériot and after flying at 700 ft, circled and came in to land. Unfortunately he struck the bank of a dyke on the airfield. The propeller hit the ground and the aircraft collapsed under him, though he was unhurt. *Flight* on 27 April reported another crash in a Gnome-Blériot when, while attempting an emergency landing, his machine was completely wrecked and he was thrown 30 ft, sustaining a dislocated wrist. On 1 October 1912 he gained his Pilot's Licence and was featured in an evocative photograph, flying a Blériot, on the front cover of *The Aeroplane* on 3 October 1912. An artist's representation of this is illustrated on the cover of this book.

Yates was born at Bromsgrove in Worcestershire on 8 March 1883 and moved to Eastbourne in about 1907 or 1908. The *Eastbourne Gazette* article of 5 July 1911 reports that he had flown at Brooklands and at Hendon. He had been present at Hendon on 25 May when the third[14] fatality in British aviation occurred; a Mr B. G. Benson, a pupil at the Valkyrie School, stalled and crashed from 200 ft[8]. Yates had just landed and was the first to get to Benson's machine and pick him up.

Yates had also been successful in motorcycle racing at Brooklands in 1910, probably with the British Motor Cycle Racing Club. Riding a 499 cc Rex motorcycle, he had won two prizes, a silver medal and a silver cup. In 1908 he had also won prizes at Aston Hill, Hertfordshire, beating C. R. Collier and H. A. Collier, two prominent early motor-cyclists. The article also claims that, while at Eastbourne, he had charge of the cars of a well-known motorist and that, in a racing car travelling between Paris and Boulogne, he attained a speed of 75 mph.

A brief mention in Cecil Lewis's *Sagittarius Rising*, a classic account of World War I flying, stimulated us to research Yates's subsequent career. Lewis wrote of being taught to fly on a Maurice Farman Longhorn at Brooklands in 1915 by a Sergeant Yates; could this have been Victor?

The answer is almost certainly 'Yes'. Yates joined the RFC, aged 30, on 27 March 1913 as a Pilot Mechanic (Service No 639). He gained his 2nd Class Army Flying Certificate at Farnborough on 1 October 1913 and qualified at the Central Flying School in 1914, subsequently serving at Farnborough as a pilot. Promoted to Sergeant, he served with 3 Squadron in France from 12 August 1914. He then returned to England and served as an instructor at Brooklands and at Northolt, teaching some 385 pupils. He was promoted Temporary Sergeant Major (Technical) on 1 January 1917 and transferred to the RAF on its formation on 1 April 1918, graded as Chief Master Mechanic (Technical).

After the war, Yates held an 'A' class Private Pilot's Licence (No 648) up to at least August 1922. In 1921, he was living at The Firs, Furnace Wood, East Grinstead.

Formation of the Eastbourne Aviation Company

Fowler had formed the Eastbourne Aviation Company on 1 December 1911, a month or so before gaining his flying certificate. Development of the site continued and the buildings included an obsolete corrugated iron church which Fowler purchased for £70. Scriptural inscriptions on the timbers were not removed, and one of them with the words 'Come, Learn' added an appropriate exhortation to the flying school pupils. Other buildings began to be erected and the Company was advertising 'tuition on genuine Blériot monoplanes, with workshop training included: special terms offered to naval officers, plus passenger flights at two guineas [£2/10s] each'.

EASTBOURNE AVIATION CO. Tuition on genuine Blériot monoplanes and Bristol biplanes. Inclusive fee for one type, £65; for both types, £90. Practical workshop instruction. Passenger and exhibition flights arranged.—For full particulars apply THE AERODROME, Eastbourne.

9. An EAC advertisement, 1913.

Most pilots appear to have taken about eight hours flying time to qualify, and the aircraft fleet was increased at this time by a machine of a new name. The records of the Bristol & Colonial Aeroplane Company Ltd, later the Bristol Aeroplane Company, at Filton include a 1912 invoice, showing a purchase by EAC of:

One Bristol Standard Military Biplane, No 119: ["Boxkite"] without motors, but with two propellers (one spare), No 409 and 410, for the sum of £275. Carriage paid, per Great Western Railway, from Temple Meads to Eastbourne.

10. A Bristol Boxkite.

This aircraft, a two-seater, which enabled dual-instruction, proved to be a stalwart of the flying school, along with two more which must have been purchased soon after. Seven pupils including Minchin, Rainey and Thomson all qualified on Boxkites (see Appendix 5).

Lieutenant Lawrence

Some excitement was generated on 26 February 1912 when a Lieutenant W. Lawrence[15] of the 7th Battalion of the Essex Regiment, on a test flight from Shoreham en route to Dover in a Blackburn Mercury monoplane, landed on the Crumbles after his engine failed. Fowler, with Yates and his mechanics, recovered and repaired the aircraft. However, Lawrence's test flight, reported in *Flight* on 30 March 1912, ended with the machine turning over on landing, injuring the pilot's arm rather badly, whereupon it was decided to return it to the Blackburn aircraft factory in Leeds for repairs.

11. Lieutenant Lawrence in his Blackburn.

Fowler's flying school went from strength to strength. In April, Fowler was reported to be testing a new EAC-built Blériot type with a 50 hp Gnome engine, while in May a 28 hp Anzani-Blériot, possibly the one that Yates had smashed in April, was ready for trial and looking smart with aluminium side shields and new wings. By June, two hangars had been erected, and a workshop of 90 × 47 ft was nearing completion. The magazine *Flight* on 28 November 1912 reported that 'quite good work had

12. The airfield in 1913, showing two Boxkites, a Morane-Saulnier, a Blériot and a biplane.

26

been done at Eastbourne. Twelve pupils have signed on, five have already taken their certificate, and several are naval men'. An *Eastbourne Gazette* article of 11 December 1912 reported that there were at the airfield a Bristol biplane, a Sommer biplane, a Blériot two-seater and a single-seater as well as in the workshop three Blériot types built by the EAC.

J. J. Hammond

In August 1912 Fowler engaged a new flying instructor, Joseph Joel Hammond, a New Zealander born at Gonville, Wanganui[16], and educated at Wellington University. He learned to fly at Reims in France and gained his Certificate (No 32) at Salisbury Plain on 22 November 1910. Hammond's previous career had included sheep-herding in Australia, gold prospecting in the Klondyke, trapping in Alaska and as a cowboy in a Wild West Show. In December 1911, he had taken two Bristol biplanes to Australia for the Bristol and Colonial Aeroplane Company and made flights over Sydney, Melbourne, Perth and other cities, thus beginning practical aviation in the Antipodes[17]. Dallas Brett, in his book, comments, perhaps unkindly, that Hammond went 'to take charge of the inefficient aerodrome at Eastbourne, and soon succeeded in producing results with the aid of a Bristol Boxkite'. Certainly *Flight* on 26 October 1912 reported that Mr Hammond had taken a holiday and so 'disappointed many people anxious to see his wonderful exhibition flights, which have made him so popular in Eastbourne'. In the *Eastbourne Gazette* of 6 November 1912 it was reported that Fowler and Hammond had, with a Mr Wadham of London,

flown over to the Willingdon Golf Links in a Blériot and a Bristol on the previous Saturday. Then *Flight* on 7 December 1912 recorded that Hammond had raced alongside a train and had also taken up a 12-bore shotgun and fired several shots at a flock of plovers. Hammond had married a local girl, Ethelwynd, of Airdale House, Seaford, soon after coming to England in 1908. He left EAC in early 1913 to return to New Zealand to start up a Flying School.

13. Joseph J. Hammond in 1910.

By 1918, he was serving as a Captain in the RAF and was a member of a British Aviation

14. Hammond in a Boxkite at the EAC.

Mission to the USA. He was killed while flying a Bristol F2B in a demonstration flight at Indianapolis on 22 September 1918, aged 31. He is buried at Crown Hill Cemetery, Indianapolis.

The Hucks Brothers

In those early days before the outbreak of war, there were two brothers, notable in early aviation, named Bentfield (Bennie) Charles Hucks and Frank Hucks.

The Hucks Starter, a device for starting aero engines without manual swinging of the propeller, was the brainchild of B. C. Hucks. He was the first British-born pilot to loop-the-loop, at Hendon Airfield in September 1913, having been taught to do so by Gustav Hamel. B. C. Hucks was also the first Briton to fly the Channel and the first to receive radio messages while in the air. Writing to the *Eastbourne Gazette* on 18 February 1914, he stated 'The future of aviation is unbounded; the fate of nations may one day be determined in the air; to this country, above all other, aerial supremacy is of vital importance, and every British citizen ought to possess some acquaintance with the possibilities and true nature of flying'. Hucks, born in Essex, died on 7 November 1918, a victim of the 'flu

No. 122681.

Certificate of Incorporation.

I hereby Certify, that THE FRANK HUCKS WATERPLANE COMPANY, LIMITED, is this day incorporated under the Companies (Consolidation) Act, 1908, and that the Company is Limited.

Given under my hand, at London, this Nineteenth day of June, One thousand nine hundred and twelve.

GEO. J. SARGENT,
Assistant Registrar of Joint Stock Companies.

Fees and Deed Stamps, £6 : 10 : 0
Stamp Duty on Capital, £12 : 10 : 0

15. Incorporation of the Frank Hucks Waterplane Company Limited.

pandemic of that year, and is buried in Highgate Cemetery, London. There are newspaper reports of his flying more than once at Eastbourne.

His brother, Frank Hucks, had registered the Frank Hucks Waterplane Company (Company Registration No 122681) in London on 19 June 1912, with the financial assistance of Charles William von Roemer, an electrical engineer of Herstmonceux, Sussex. The authorised share capital was £5,000, to be issued in £1 shares. Hucks, of 2a Adelaide Road, South Hampstead, London, was named as Secretary with one £1 share and von Roemer, of Lime Park, Herstmonceux, as a Director with 500 shares. In addition, three times that year von Roemer subscribed capital in the form of debentures: £2,500 on 25 June, £1,393 on 20 September and £450 on 29 October.

16. Charles W. de Roemer (formerly von Roemer) in 1960.

17. A Henry Farman seaplane off Eastbourne.

Hucks toured seaside resorts, including Eastbourne, with two 70 hp Gnome-engined Henry Farman seaplanes, offering flights for adventurous passengers on a fare-paying basis though never, so far as is known, holding a flying certificate. Flights of this nature were no novelty at Eastbourne, since the author H. G. Wells had his first flight in a Farman seaplane at the town from near the Queen's Hotel in August 1912, of which he later wrote[18] 'the waterplane in which I soared over Eastbourne this morning with Mr Grahame-White was as steady as a motor-car running on asphalt'. Between May and September 1912, the *Daily Mail* pioneered these waterplane 'Circuit of Britain' tours, which also offered the carriage of postcards, overprinted with a suitable cachet, for a small fee.

About this time, Frank Hucks and Fowler got to know each other – there was great camaraderie in early flying days – and from that association further developments in Eastbourne aviation soon occurred. At an Extraordinary Meeting of the Frank Hucks Waterplane Company Limited, held at the Queen's Hotel, Eastbourne, on Saturday 18 January 1913, the name was changed to the Eastbourne Aviation Company Limited, and the change was registered on 24 February 1913, under the guidance of the Company's solicitors, Messrs Hingley & Roll of Midland

No. 122681.

Certificate of Change of Name.

I hereby Certify, that THE FRANK HUCKS WATERPLANE COMPANY, LIMITED having, with the sanction of a SPECIAL RESOLUTION of the said Company, and with the approval of the BOARD OF TRADE, changed its name, is now called EASTBOURNE AVIATION COMPANY, LIMITED, and I have entered such name on the Register accordingly.

Given under my hand at London, this Twentyfourth day of February, One thousand nine hundred and thirteen.

GEO. J. SARGENT,
Assistant Registrar of Joint Stock Companies.

18. The Change of Name.

Bank Chambers, Eastbourne. The authorised share capital was increased to £15,000, made up of 5,000 £1 ordinary shares and 10,000 5% Preference Shares, also of £1. Fowler and von Roemer were elected Permanent Directors, with Frank Hucks as Secretary and Fowler Managing Director. Another shareholder, with 1,000 shares, was Rowland Edward Brian Hunt, gentleman, of Baschurch, Park Avenue in Hampden Park, Eastbourne, who later became a pupil at the airfield, qualifying on 22 December 1913 with Certificate No 715, without, it was said, any favouritism because of his shareholding. The registered office was recorded as the Aerodrome, Eastbourne.

The amalgamation of the two companies heralded the commencement of seaplane flights, using Henry Farman seaplanes, which operated from the beach to the west of the pier as well as from other local resorts. This must also have been the inspiration for the building of the Seaplane Base. According to the *Eastbourne Gazette* of 27 August 1913, flights

The Companies (Consolidation) Act, 1908.

COMPANY LIMITED BY SHARES.

Memorandum

AND

Articles of Association

OF

Eastbourne Aviation Company, Limited.

(A Private Company adopting Table A with modifications.)

Incorporated the 19th day of June, 1912.

HINGLEY & ROLL,
MIDLAND BANK CHAMBERS,
EASTBOURNE.

19. Memorandum and Articles of Association.

20. An EAC Henry Farman seaplane on the beach at Eastbourne.

had been given to people in Eastbourne and Bexhill in a seaplane, one passenger being a Miss Gwynne, who was 71 years of age at the time; others included J. Dennison of 28 Upperton Gardens, Eastbourne, and Dorothy M. Jay, daughter of the Revd W. P. Jay of St Anne's Church, Eastbourne.

By this time Frank Hucks[19] had moved to a house: Craigneuk, at 75 Willingdon Road, Eastbourne and by 6 April 1914 his wife, Blanche, had become a preference shareholder in the sum of £250.

The Seaplane Base

The Company now leased land and owned seaplanes, and thus required buildings to house them. This was undertaken on the Crumbles, on land leased from Baron Willingdon of Ratton, in March 1913. The rent was £10 per annum rising over 14 years to £30. The Seaplane Base consisted of a large hangar and other buildings (see Appendix 2) built at the seaward end of Lottbridge Drove,

21. Aerial view of the Seaplane Base.

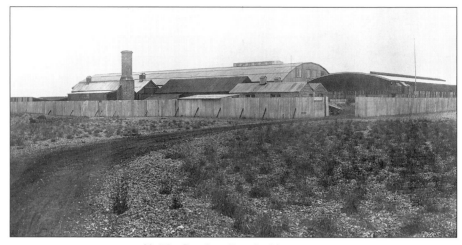

22. The Seaplane Base looking south.

slightly to the west of the site of today's Sovereign Leisure Centre, with a turntable and launching track down to the high water line. Eastbourne thus became one of the few airfields in England with land and sea facilities.

The EAC Aircraft

In 1912 the Company had acquired the services of an able Swiss engineer and designer in Emil Louis Gassler. Born at Koblenz in the Aargau, northern Switzerland, in August 1888, Gassler came to Eastbourne from Shoreham Airfield where he had been a pupil at the Chanter School until it was destroyed by fire on 28 February 1912. He

23. Emil Gassler in 1912.

qualified at Eastbourne for his Pilot's Certificate (No 350) on 29 October 1912, but, more importantly to the EAC, Gassler's arrival heralded the commencement of aeroplane production at Eastbourne (see Appendix 3). His designs formed the basis of the four main EAC machines, though there can be little doubt that he worked in close consultation with Fowler. The article in *Air Pictorial* of March 1979 suggests that EAC produced three early aircraft, a 'new type monoplane' in the spring of 1912, a Blériot with a 50 hp engine in April and a small biplane with a 35 hp Anzani engine in 1913 which lifted only about 4 ft on trial, with the top wing collapsing on its landing. (The *Eastbourne Gazette* article of 11 December 1912 mentions three EAC-built Blériot types.) We have no firm documentary evidence for the production of these machines, though a 1913 photograph of the airfield clearly shows a tractor biplane together with two Boxkites, a Morane-Saulnier and a Blériot (see illustration on page 26). In November 1913, Fowler sold three of the Blériots, the EAC Monoplane, a Bristol Biplane (presumably a Boxkite) and a Gnome engine for £4,000.

The EAC Monoplane

The first truly successful design was in 1913 and was to be called the E.L.G. after its designer, Emil Gassler. It was a single-seater tractor monoplane (see Appendix 4) powered by a three-cylinder 35 hp Anzani radial engine driving a 7 ft diameter Rapid propeller. The engine was mounted in the nose of a rectangular section fuselage, metal-covered as far back as the rear of the cockpit and tapered from a deep belly beneath the cockpit to a knife edge at the tail. The aircraft, which was described and illustrated at length in *Flight* of 3 May 1913, incorporated a one-piece elevator operating below a cut-out in the rudder which was braced by a strut to the top of the fuselage. A cabane, or pyramid of struts, was placed under the belly of the fuselage in order to provide a point of attachment for the flying wires, which would thus be insulated from undercarriage shocks. The 29 ft span wings, with an area of 135 sq ft,

24. The EAC Monoplane – ¾ view.

35

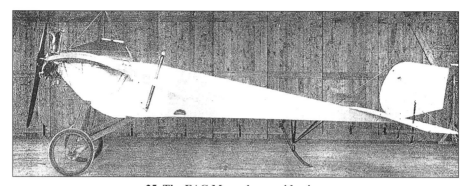

25. The EAC Monoplane – side view.

were mounted just below the upper longerons. The aircraft was the first monoplane to employ inter-connected ailerons instead of the more usual wing-warping, so eliminating twisting strains and giving improved flying characteristics. Landing strains were taken by wires attached to a single A-shaped pylon in front of the cockpit. The undercarriage axle was sprung by means of rubber shock absorbers. A cruising speed of 50 mph was claimed. The anticipated private sales were not forthcoming and, despite the favourable write-up in *Flight*, only one was built. The aircraft, however, proved useful as a trainer. According to Dallas Brett, the design was an improvement on that of the Dyott monoplane, which was completed early in 1913 and which enjoyed a series of successful exhibition flights in the USA in 1913. In November 1913, while taking part in a London–Brighton handicap race, the Dyott was forced to land on Beachy Head and was blown over onto its back.

Lieutenant Hunt's Biplane

The EAC monoplane was followed by a single-seater biplane, with a 50 hp Gnome engine, built in February 1914 for the express use of Lieutenant R. E. B. Hunt (see opposite) for exhibition flying. It was a single-seater tractor biplane, fitted with a 50 hp Gnome engine. Unfortunately, no layout drawings exist for the machine, which was reported to have a cruising speed of 65 mph. *Flight* featured the machine on 7 March 1914, showing a photograph of Hunt in the pilot's seat and Gassler standing alongside him (Appendix 6). Hunt is reported to have taken the aircraft with him when he joined the RFC in 1914. Only one was built.

26. Lieutenant Hunt's Biplane.

The EAC Military Biplane

Fowler's next venture was to build a military biplane, which received a substantial write-up in *Flight* of 21 March and 18 April 1914 and which was exhibited at the Olympia Aero Show in March of that year, where it received favourable comment from King George V (see Appendix 7). Fowler staked much on this show, renting a 50 ft square stand next to that of Louis Blériot. Equipped with an 80 hp Gnome engine, the aircraft was

27. The EAC Military Biplane at Olympia.

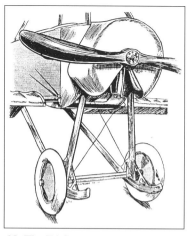

28. The EAC Military Biplane – the engine cowling and undercarriage.

a tandem two-seater tractor biplane with a rather long square section fuselage carrying an 80 hp Gnome engine partly enclosed by an aluminium cowl and driving an 8 ft 6 in diameter propeller. The wings were of unequal length, the lower pair shorter than the upper, while a slight taper was incorporated into the leading edges. To improve visibility for the crew, the lower wing roots and the upper section were left open. The undercarriage incorporated short forward projecting skids and was sprung by means of rubber cords.

Special features included robust construction combined with light weight, ease of erection and dismantling and, unusually, a starting handle in front of the pilot, making it possible to start the engine without swinging the propeller, so enabling the machine to be restarted without outside assistance in the event of forced landings. With an unladen weight of 950 lb, the aircraft had a top speed of 75 mph and a landing speed of 50 mph. Unfortunately for Fowler, it was overshadowed by the Avro Scout and the Bristol Scout, as well as the Sopwith Tabloid, which was not exhibited. Sadly the aircraft did not receive official endorsement and again only one was built.

29. The EAC Military Biplane at Olympia.

The Circuit of Britain Seaplane

The final aircraft to be designed and built by EAC was a massive two-seater tractor biplane, intended to become entry No 5, flown by Fowler, in the 1914 *Daily Mail* Circuit of Britain Contest for seaplanes (see Appendix 8). The aircraft was to be sponsored jointly by Fowler and Frank Hucks. The ambitious design embodied a 100 hp Green engine mounted inside the fuselage driving a pair of 8 ft 6 in tractor propellers through inclined shafts and bevel gearing. There was a two-seat, side-by-side cockpit in the nose of the fuselage. The 54 ft wings were of conventional parallel form with the trailing edges slightly longer than the leading and large ailerons incorporated in the wing tips.

30. The EAC Circuit Seaplane at the Seaplane Base.

The aeroplane was supported in the water by a pair of floats set 12 ft apart; these, at 19 ft in length, were judged long enough to avoid the need for wing or tail floats. They also incorporated a novel feature in the form of two welded pipes running from front to rear whose object was to break the partial vacuum which tended to impede such machines from leaving the surface.

The principle of the drive through two inclined shafts was attractive, but less than satisfactory in practice because of the tendency of the struts to distort when full power was applied. There is no evidence of the aircraft undergoing flying trials and it was in fact being modified when war broke out and the contest for which it was designed was cancelled. By the time that *Flight* published its usual reports on the new aircraft on 4 September and again on 11 December 1914, Britain was already at war with Germany and the *Daily Mail* Circuit of Britain was cancelled. EAC's seaplane, which may well never have flown, was broken up. Dallas Brett gives it scant respect, stating that 'the EAC entry was in the nature of a freak, and need not be described here'.

Gustav Hamel

Gustav Hamel – of immortal fame in air history – certainly knew Eastbourne Airfield well. He flew there on several occasions, looping-the-loop to delight the crowds, once in brilliant moonlight over the end of the pier, landing with the remark that he had enjoyed seeing the lights of France during his manoeuvres.

Hamel was born on 25 June 1889, of Scandinavian ancestry. He was naturalised British, and educated at Westminster School and Caius College, Cambridge. An ex-mechanic of Eastbourne Airfield once assured Gerald

31. Gustav Hamel.

Newson that Gustav Hamel was 'a bit of a one for the ladies'. Like McArdle earlier in the story, Hamel trained with Blériot at Issy-les-Moulineaux, passing his test at Pau in France. When Hamel first flew at Eastbourne in February 1914, in a Morane-Saulnier monoplane, it cost two shillings [10p] to watch him from in front of the hangers on the airfield, or one shilling [5p] from the nearby higher ground. Sadly, he lost his life in the Channel on 23 May 1914 while flying a new racing Morane monoplane from Boulogne to Hendon to take part in the Hendon to Brooklands Aerial Derby on 24 May.

Commander Samson

On 7 March 1914, Commander Charles Samson, RN, who achieved considerable fame in the war that was shortly to come and who features later in our story, landed a 140 hp Short biplane at the airfield. With a wing-span of 60 ft, this was the largest aircraft yet to have come to Eastbourne[20]. Samson was not only the first Royal Naval officer to qualify as a pilot but also the first to take off from a ship at sea. Adverse weather conditions delayed Samson's departure from Eastbourne until 9 March.

Rowland Ding and the Princess

On 21 May 1914, Mr Rowland Ding, accompanied by the Princess Lowenstein-Wertheim (who features later in this story – see page 59), landed at Eastbourne at 8.45 am in a new Handley-Page biplane. Although Ding had only passed his test on 28 April, Mr Handley-Page had already nominated him as his pilot for the Aerial Derby which was to be flown on 24 May. Due to fog over the Channel, Mr Ding and his passenger had to spend most of the day at the Eastbourne Airfield. Then, taking off at 3.30 pm, they arrived at Calais at 4.20 pm, a very fast crossing.

Fowler's Marriage

Before we reach the Great War, we take a diversion to mention an event of great importance in the life of Frederick Bernard Fowler – his marriage. To be precise, his first marriage, on Saturday 11 October 1913, to Josephine Gertrude Oakey, daughter of Herbert Oakey and his wife Fanny, whose family firm was a well-known manufacturer of glass-paper and abrasives. They lived in a house named Avoca[21] in Old Wish Road, which now forms part of Eastbourne College.

Josephine Oakey had been born on 20 November 1884 at Streatham, south-west London, where the family owned a fine house, Caton Lodge, overlooking Streatham Common.

The Marriage Certificate contains two interesting features. The first is the description of Fowler's profession as 'Aeroplanist', and the second is that Fowler's address is shown as Borough House, Old Town, Eastbourne, although it will be recalled that he lived at Avalona,

32. Mr and Mrs Fowler in 1913.

57 Watts Lane, with his parents. Ordinarily he would have been married at the church of his own residential parish, which was St Michael and All Angels. Like many couples before them, the Fowlers chose the larger and more fashionable Parish Church of St Mary in Old Town, where they were married by the Vicar of Eastbourne, Canon William C. Streatfield, father of Noel Streatfield, the novelist. Borough House, not far from St Mary's Church, was a rather upper-class lodging house kept by a Miss M. Hart. Whether Fowler stayed there while his banns were being called, or whether he lodged a suitcase there to meet the spirit of the law of residential qualification, his address on the Marriage Certificate is thus explained.

33. The Fowlers about to start their honeymoon.

34. Belhurst, near Herstmonceux.

Press reports of the occasion show that the best man was Walter de Burley Wood[22], who also acted as witness. The other witness was recorded as E. Hines. The *Eastbourne Gazette* of 15 October 1913 notes that the wedding was a quiet affair in the morning, that a guard of honour was provided by Fowler's mechanics, and that the honeymoon was to be a motoring tour in Britain using a new De Dion Bouton motorcar, a present from the bride's parents. The same *Eastbourne Gazette* article includes a substantial list of wedding presents. The guest list included a Pleasance Oswald, whose mother was an Oakey and thus related to the bride. Pleasance re-appears in the Fowler story fairly soon.

Fowler and his wife moved to a delightful house named Belhurst[23] in the Parish of Wartling, near Herstmonceux, where he often landed his aircraft in fields opposite the house. By 1924 they had three daughters, two of whom were alive in the 1980s, one in Bury St Edmunds, the other in Stowmarket. The youngest died in Canada in 1960. Sadly, the marriage failed and Mrs Fowler, with the three girls, left Belhurst in 1925 and moved to France. The rest of their lives need not concern us here, save to add that the divorce took place in 1926. Some four years later, Fowler married Pleasance Oswald, named above as a guest at his first marriage, and known to the family circle as 'Cubby'.

His first wife died in 1966, and Pleasance in 1978.

1. See Appendix 9.

2. The Special Committee established on 25 February 1909 consisted of Alderman Keay (Chairman), Alderman Duke and Councillors Herridge and Sharp.

3. The Aviation Committee established on 4 October 1909 consisted of the Mayor (Alderman Martin), Alderman Keay, Councillors Major Cooke, Fox, Harding, Simmons, Thornton, Messrs C. de Broe, Roland Burke (Professional Agent to the Duke of Devonshire) and landowners C. Davies Gilbert and F. Freeman Thomas, MP. At the first meeting of the Committee on 14 October 1909, Mr Roland Burke was elected Chairman and Councillor Simmons Vice-Chairman.

4. *The Christchurch Times*, 28 November 1958. (Fowler spent the latter part of his life living near to Christchurch, at that time in Hampshire, but which is now a part of Dorset.)

5. New College (1872–1904) occupied buildings in Compton Place Road, later to become Temple Grove School, now the Dental Practice Agency.

6. The Thornycroft 20 hp was an advanced car for its day, with a 3558 cc overhead valve four cylinder engine and shaft drive. A 1904 model is at the Heritage Motor Centre at Gaydon, Warwickshire.

7. Ministry of Defence letters of 6 and 15 June 1979.

8. Brett, R. Dallas (1934): *History of British Aviation 1908–1914*.

9. *Eastbourne Gazette,* 12 July 1911.

10. Butcher, R.: Bernard Fowler – the Tin Shed Pioneer: *RAF Flying Review*, Vol XV, No 1, September 1959.

11. *Flight*, on 11 October 1913, referred to the coastguards sending a rescue boat.

12. *Flight*, 20 January 1912.

13. Flying certificates were known variously as RAeC (Royal Aeronautical Club) certificates, licences, tickets, brevets, etc.

14. The first two fatalities were the Hon C. S. Rolls (of Rolls-Royce fame) on 11 July 1910 and Cecil Grace on 22 December 1910.

15. *Eastbourne Gazette*, 28 February 1912.

16. Commonwealth War Graves Commission (*Eastbourne Gazette* of 9 October 1912 refers to Hammond as having been born at Feilding, Rangitiker).

17. *Flight*, 16 March 1912.

18. Wells, H. G. (1914): *An Englishman looks at the World.*

19. Frank Hucks served in HMS *President*, in the Engineer-in-Chief's Department of the Royal Navy at Deptford, and was promoted Acting Engineer Lieutenant Commander on 15 July 1916. He was discharged in November 1919. A former airfield employee recalled that Hucks' furniture came to Eastbourne Airfield for storage and, piece by piece, vanished at the hands of sundry individuals. Mrs Hucks continued to be involved as a shareholder for a while after the war.

20. Ashworth, C. (1990): *Action Stations 9: Military Airfields of the Central South and South East.*

21. Avoca was acquired by Eastbourne College in 1931 as the Headmaster's house, which it remains to this day.

22. *Flight*, 21 June 1913, records that a Mr Walter Wood was a local observer appointed by the Royal Aeronautical Club, and that during June he was given a cross-country flight to Fowler's house and back.

23. Belhurst had been the Dower House to the Windmill Hill Estate and is now a private residence.

The Men that Fowler taught to fly

Twenty men obtained their Royal Aeronautical Club Certificate, or brevet, at Eastbourne Airfield (see Appendix 5) before it was turned over for use by the RNAS in 1914. We have dealt elsewhere in this narrative with the lives of three of these: Fowler, Yates and Gassler. Of the remaining 17, 13 went on to serve with the RNAS or RFC and later the RAF. Another, Charles Oxlade, remained on naval service and another, Frederick Bevis, so far as is known, returned to serve with the Indian Army. Of the later careers of Dennis Gwynne and William Roberts, nothing has been found.

35. **Aviators and pupils at the aerodrome, June 1913.** *Seated:* **S. J. Fill, F. Hucks, F. B. Fowler.** *Standing:* **W. S. Roberts, L. Fry, E. Gassler, R. F. Morkill.** *In the pilot's seat:* **T. A. Rainey.**

To undergo flying training in 1912 and 1913, when aviation was so unproven, must have required a special brand of courage. A number of the Eastbourne pilots experienced hair-raising escapades prior to qualifying; some achieved high rank and served with distinction in the post-war RAF; several were decorated for gallantry during the war, and inevitably there were those who gave their lives in that conflict. At least one served in WW2. Three, Brown, Foggin and Playfair, are buried in the cemeteries in Flanders that are so beautifully maintained by the

Commonwealth War Graves Commission. We have visited and photographed each of their graves and include those of Brown and Cyril Foggin in this chapter. Details of orders, awards and decorations that are referenced in the book are given at Appendix 9.

So it is as a mark of respect for their lives that we have researched and recorded here as much as we have been able to ascertain from records in the public domain. For ease of reference, we list them in alphabetical order.

36. Frederick Bevis in 1913.

Frederick George Bevis was born at Naina Tal, India, on 18 August 1893. The son of W. G. Bevis of Pembury, Staveley Road, Eastbourne, he attended Eastbourne College as a home boarder from 1908 to 1910. He obtained his Certificate (No 629) at EAC on 13 September 1913 and was commissioned into the Indian Army in 1914, serving as a lieutenant with the 87th Punjabis, attached to the 97th Deccan Infantry. There is evidence that he survived the war and was serving as a Captain in the 2nd Punjab Regiment in the 1920s.

Reginald John Bone was born at Dorking on 2 October 1888. A lieutenant, RN, serving in submarines, he came to Eastbourne in 1912 to learn to fly. His own record of these events appeared in *Cross and Cockade Great Britain* in 1978 and describes graphically his experience[1]:

'While my submarine was in dock at Sheerness I was able to get away at the weekends and, in 1912, started a course of instruction at the Eastbourne Aviation School of Flying which at that time was equipped with Blériot monoplanes only. These were difficult for pupils to keep straight on the ground. The first process in learning to fly was therefore a series of straight rolls on the ground. These were carried out on an old 25 hp Anzani Blériot that was no longer regarded as fit to fly. The instructions to the pupil were to throttle back at once if the aircraft left the ground. These straight rolls were carried out only under conditions of absolute calm, *viz*, shortly after dawn and in the evenings. The next phase was to be taken up in a dual control Blériot.

One calm evening when I was doing one of my straight rolls an unexpected gust of wind lifted the old Blériot up to 50 or 60 ft, heading for the gasworks. With no knowledge of piloting, except what I had learnt from listening to pilots talk, I contrived to complete a half circuit and by some fluke made a faultless landing whereupon the old Anzani coughed and died away.

Nobody could have been more pleased with himself than me and nobody could have been more angry than my instructor [J. J. Hammond]. He ran out to the aircraft and told me that I had disobeyed his orders, and that my flying instruction was terminated. "Get off the aerodrome and don't come back." However, I took no notice of that and some weeks later – after dual control instruction – I took my Aviator's Certificate on a pusher Bristol Biplane' [RAeC Certificate No 627 on 16 August 1913].

37. Lt R. J. Bone, RN, in 1913.

Bone enjoyed a distinguished career, serving in both world wars and in the years between, gaining a CB, CBE and DSO.

Entering the Royal Navy as a Midshipman in February 1904, he served as Sub-Lieutenant on HMS *Foam*, a destroyer, in 1908, with HMS *Dolphin*, the Portsmouth submarine base and then in submarine C1 until 1913. After qualifying as a pilot, he was seconded to the RNAS, joining the fourth course at the Central Flying School, Upavon, in September 1913. Appointed Flying Officer on 17 December 1913, Flight Lieutenant, RNAS on 1 July 1914, Flight Commander on 22 February 1915 and Squadron Commander on 30 June 1916, he served at RNAS, Isle of Grain, Yarmouth, HMS *Empress*, Dunkirk, Eastchurch and South Shields.

On 3 February 1915, a Dunkirk seaplane flight was established under the general command of the redoubtable Commander C. R. Samson, RNAS, with Bone one of the four pilots. On 11 February, Samson planned a bombing raid on German-held coastal ports and assembled no less than twenty-two assorted aeroplanes, flying from various airfields. In Samson's own words: 'Bone carried out a splendid flight. Reaching Blankenberge unperceived, he hit the railway station there with a 100 lb bomb, with corresponding good results, killing a number of German soldiers.'

During his time at Eastchurch, Bone was given command of a small sub-unit at Detling, near Maidstone. It was a time when German hit-and-run raiders were making daylight bombing attacks on the Kentish seaside towns. In Bone's own words:

'One Sunday at Detling I put some sandwiches and coffee into my Nieuport [3964] and went to a little airfield we had at Westgate. There I put the Nieuport on the airfield in position for take off and ate my sandwiches. German [Friedrichshaven] seaplanes arrived at a good altitude at lunchtime as I expected – bombed Margate [and Ramsgate and Dover] and killed some [twelve] civilians before making out to sea.

I was off in time to sight one of the enemy planes – my problem was to keep up with it while climbing to its altitude. Once at the same altitude my Nieuport had superior performance. This involved a very long pursuit in the direction of Zeebrugge but finally I was able to get close up under the seaplane and delivered a good burst from my machine gun. The enemy pilot instantly went into a steep dive – so steep we nearly collided. Thereafter I saw him go down and alight on the water.

The incident was built up by the Press into a tremendous affair because it was the first time contact had been made with these "hit-and-run" raids. The story of my wait at Westgate also made good material.

A certain amount of annoyance was generated by all this publicity among RNAS pilots at Eastchurch and Dover; but they could not possibly have got in touch with the raiders from these aerodromes. This was counter-balanced by the joy among the non-flying senior naval officers in charge of the RNAS area which resulted in my being given an "immediate" DSO which I probably had not really earned.'

The award of the DSO came on 7 April 1916.

After a brief spell at the Admiralty in July 1916, Bone joined No 2 Wing of the Aegean Group in October 1916, moving on to the Mudros Airship Station in October 1916. By March 1918, now an Acting Wing Commander, RNAS, he was employed at the Ministry of Munitions. He joined the North Russian Expeditionary Force to Murmansk in 1919 and on 1 March 1920 was gazetted Wing Commander, RAF, with a permanent commission.

Appointed Inspector of Recruiting in June 1921, he next served at Calshot 1923–25 and Karachi, India (now Pakistan), 1925–29. Promoted Group Captain in July 1929, he was Air Attaché at the British Embassy in Paris 1929–31. He was placed on the retired list in April 1934, with the award of a CB.

He subsequently served in the Air Ministry in 1935 and was lent for duty as Director General of Civil Aviation for the Egyptian Government 1936–39.

He rejoined the RAF for the 1939–45 war, joining Coastal Command on 4 September 1939 and then reverted to the retired list on 14 January 1941. After a spell with the RAF Station at Pembroke Dock, later in 1941 he became RAF Civil Defence Liaison Officer in the Midlands. After the war he was Civil Air Attaché to British Embassies in Nanking, Bangkok and Manila up to 1951.

Bone married in 1942 and during the 1950s worked for Lucas Engineering. In the 1960s he travelled the country in a sports car as a sales representative for a company which made the first automatic car wash in the UK. He eventually retired in 1970 at the age of 82, when he was living at Pitmaston Court, Wake Green Road, Moseley, Birmingham. He died on 29 August 1972.

1. Bone, R. J.: A Record of Good Luck: *Cross and Cockade Great Britain*, Vol 9, No 1, 1978.

Alexander Clive Garden Brown was born on 19 August 1890 at Dwindridgemuir, Lanarkshire, the son of Alexander and Charlotte Brown of Strathwell Park, Whitwell, on the Isle of Wight. He was educated at Bradfield College (1903–05) and at the Britannia Royal Naval College, Dartmouth. Commissioned as a Sub-Lieutenant, RN, he came to EAC in 1912, gaining Certificate No 398 on 21 January 1913. Brown must have transferred to the RFC at some time and later to the RAF on its formation on 1 April 1918.

Nothing is known of his service until 1918 when he three times appears flying with 48 Squadron.

38. Sub-Lt A. C. G. Brown, RN, in 1913.

39. Brown's grave at Heath Cemetery.

The first occasion was on 22 March 1918 when he was serving as a Second Lieutenant, RFC, flying a Bristol F2B, (C4606) with Second Lieutenant G. C. Bartlett. He dived at a group of five enemy aircraft, firing short bursts. One enemy aircraft flew into the ground and Brown was wounded in this action. On 15 April, flying with Second Lieutenant W. Hart, his machine was damaged while on low-level reconnaissance. On 3 May 1918, flying a similar aircraft (C814) with Corporal A. W. Sainsbury, he was again wounded, this time coming down over enemy lines[1]. He died of wounds at Herteville on 6–7 May as a prisoner of war.

He is buried at Heath Military Cemetery, Harbonnières, France, a few miles south of Albert.

1. Henshaw, T. (1995): *The Sky their Battlefield.*

40. S. J. V. Fill in 1913.

Samuel John Valentine (or Vincent) Fill was born on 5 October 1879 at South Shields, County Durham, and qualified at EAC on 3 August 1913 with Certificate No 578.

A marine engineer, he was commissioned Temporary Lieutenant, RNVR, on 26 December 1915 and served on HMS *Empress* from January 1916 until early 1917. He then served in the Air Department at the Admiralty (April 1917) and at Crystal Palace, being promoted Temporary

Lieutenant Commander early in 1918. The same year he transferred to the RAF on its formation with the rank of Major.

He was awarded the OBE in the *London Gazette* of 3 June 1916.

Cyril Edgar Foggin was born on 2 November 1891 at South Gosforth, Newcastle upon Tyne, the son of William and Jane Foggin of Haddicks Mill Road, South Gosforth. By June 1911, he was apprenticed to Maison Borel Morane, designers and builders of aircraft, at Vidarnée, Oise, in France. By 1912 he had purchased and was flying his own plane, a Blackburn monoplane with a 50 hp Gnome engine. (This aircraft is now owned by the Shuttleworth Collection at Old Warden Aerodrome, Beds, where it is maintained in flying condition[1].)

41. Cyril Foggin in 1912.

Later that year he joined EAC for flying training and it was there he had his first documented[2] accident. While flying an Anzani-engined Blériot on 24 September 1912, he lost control in strong winds at 60 ft over the site of the recently demolished Martello Tower at St Anthony's Hill. As *Flight* of 28 September had it: 'getting up to 100 ft, he commenced a series of most alarming evolutions, ending in a spiral dive. His machine struck the ground almost vertically and was smashed to pieces'. He crashed onto the grassy slope on the Langney side of the hill.

42. Foggin's 1912 Blackburn – the earliest British aircraft still flying.

Workmen nearby raced over to the crash, expecting to find him dead, but instead he was very much alive. He attributed his survival to his thick leather flying helmet, which had been specially made for him by T. A. Larkin, the Saddler, of South Street, Eastbourne. Interviewed by the *Eastbourne Gazette*, Foggin was reported as saying: 'When I felt I was going to fall I took my feet off the controls and rolled myself up. I was ready for the shock and took it all on my head. If it had not been for the helmet I should have split my head open. Although I felt I was falling and that my end was near, the dipping was a most pleasant sensation. The helmet, which struck against the front of the machine, has a dent which is two inches long but not deep. When the monoplane struck the ground I was underneath, but I was able to crawl out. I heard people coming up, saying "He's dead, he's dead". The machine is a total wreck, and the force with which it struck the ground is shown by the depth to which some of the woodwork entered the soil. I had a slight headache and was a bit shaken. Otherwise I was quite all right'.

Foggin passed his Certificate (No 349) on 29 October 1912 on a Blériot monoplane. He sold his Blackburn in June 1913 and by September had joined the aviation department at Armstrong Whitworth. Then, volunteering for war service, he recorded his civilian profession as 'aviator'.

Foggin went on to serve as a pilot with 1 Squadron, RFC, in France. On 27 April 1916[3], flying a Nieuport, he brought down an enemy Albatross near Bailleul, sustaining a wound which led to the loss of his left eye. On 22 August 1917[4], by now a Captain, he was serving with 56(T) Squadron at London Colney on home defence duties, where he flew a Spad (A8817) on sorties against Gotha raids. By March/April 1918, now a Major, Foggin was posted as an instructor to No 1 School of Aerial Fighting at Ayr Racecourse, Strathclyde, in Scotland, under the command of Colonel Lionel Rees, VC, MC, (who had been educated at Eastbourne College). This was a school of advanced aerial fighter training which existed between 17 September 1917 and 10 May 1918. A contemporary report[5] records, 'All the flying here is stunting and we have service machines. Every time we go up, we are supposed to find another machine and have a dog-fight with it. The Colonel stays in the air a lot and is the best at scrapping – he and Foggin. . . . Foggin is a wonderful pilot and only has one eye'.

43. St Riquier Military Cemetery: Foggin's and Scholke's graves (3rd and 4th from the right).

In May 1918, Foggin was classified as permanently unfit for general service and transferred to a staff appointment with the temporary rank of Major. He was also recorded as having flown 2,500 hours in eleven different machines.

He was killed in France, at the age of 26, on the night of 29/30 July 1918 in a motor-car accident together with Captain Owen Scholke, MC, of 60 Squadron. The Crossley car was being driven by the Commanding Officer of 60 Squadron, Major Cyril Crowe, MC, who was court-martialled, severely reprimanded and lost seniority. A month later Crowe was given command of 85 Squadron.

Foggin is buried alongside Captain Scholke in the military cemetery at St Riquier, near Hesdin in northern France.

1. Jackson, A. J.: *Blackburn Aircraft since 1909:* the second edition questions whether the Shuttleworth aircraft is Foggin's.
2. *Eastbourne Gazette,* 25 September 1912.
3. Cole, C. (ed) (1969): *Royal Flying Corps Communiques 1915–1916.*
4. Cole, C. and Cheesman E. F. (1984): *The Air Defence of Britain 1914–1918.*
5. Spring, E. (1927): *War Birds – Diary of an Unknown Aviator.*

44. Dennis Gwynne in 1914.

Dennis Gwynne, who was born at Manchester on 21 June 1895, passed his test on the EAC biplane at Eastbourne with Certificate No 829 on 30 June 1914. Nothing is known of his subsequent career, though he reported an accommodation address at North Shore, Sydney, Australia, when recording his RAeC Certificate.

Rowland Edward Brian Hunt, known as 'Brian', was born on 21 May 1892, the son of the MP for the Ludlow Division of Shropshire, whose name, confusingly, was also Rowland Hunt. His father owned a house, Baschurch, in Park Avenue, Hampden Park, Eastbourne, between 1913 and 1915. This may have been purchased for his son's use while in Eastbourne, for he gave the military authorities an address in Ladbroke Gardens, Notting Hill, London. Hunt had been gazetted Second Lieutenant, the 3rd Battalion, the Kings Shropshire Light Infantry on 13 July 1910, and was promoted Lieutenant on 13 May 1913.

He came to Eastbourne as a pupil in 1913 and had three crashes during his training, the cost of which were met by his father. In February, he was making a cross-country flight when he had an engine failure over Polegate, the aircraft canting to one side and striking the ground with some force, buckling the fuselage and smashing both wings. He emerged unhurt, apart from a severe shaking.

45. Lt 'Brian' Hunt with a Blériot.

The second, on 25 November, was a pancake from a height of about 20 ft in a Blériot, which was slightly damaged. The third, on the same day, was when he was taking the first part of his tests for the RAeC brevet. He had successfully completed five figures of eight, when an inlet valve in the engine stuck, the engine stopped, and the aircraft went into a dive. Suddenly the engine restarted and Hunt

46. Hunt's crash on the house roof.

tried to bank round the aircraft sheds to land. As he came in, the inlet valve stuck again, and he had no alternative but to pancake onto the roof of a house in St Anthony's Avenue that was under construction. He escaped injury, but both the house and the aircraft were badly damaged. The *Sussex Daily News* of 26 November 1913, reporting on the two accidents, remarked 'that the occupiers of the damaged house are at present away from home'.

Hunt passed his Certificate (No 715) on 22 December 1913 on the EAC biplane (or possibly on the biplane that was built to his order). He took this machine with him when he joined the RFC.

He was promoted to Captain in June 1915, attached to 7 Squadron, RFC, in France. On 13 July[1], while flying a Voisin LA (1898), he was in combat near Comines.

Hunt was reported missing on 21 July 1915[2]. Piloting an RE5 (678) with Lieutenant F. H. Jackson as observer, on a reconnaissance trip between St Omer and Ghent, the engine failed at 5,000 ft, due to enemy fire. At 06.10 he made a forced landing at Wuijckhuysepolder, Sluiskil in Holland, where he set fire to and burnt the aircraft. Hunt and Jackson were interned in Holland until their repatriation on 21 November 1918.

By 1919 Hunt was living at Wayside, Woldingham, Surrey.

1. Henshaw, T. (1995): *The Sky their Battlefield.*

2. *Ibid.* and van Dorssen, H. & Gerdessen, F. in *Cross and Cockade Great Britain*, Vol 16, No 1, 1985.

Frank William Lerwill was born at Newport, Monmouthshire, on 27 September 1881[1], the son of a jeweller and watchmaker. After serving as a junior officer in the Army in the South African War, Lerwill spent some years in Argentina where he met and married his wife. During his absence, his father had established a jewellery business at 7 Cornfield Road, Eastbourne (1904–1913). So, on his return to England in 1912, he decided to learn to fly at the EAC. There, flying a Boxkite, he gained his Certificate (No 359) on 12 November of that year[2].

Volunteering for service with the RFC, he attended the Central Flying School in November/December 1914. Then in January 1915 he joined 2 Squadron at Merville in France. Soon, as a Lieutenant, he transferred to 9 Squadron and was injured in a crash[3] on 12 March 1916. Taking off to test a newly overhauled BE2c (2115) with a young soldier, Private H. Thacker of the 8th Battalion, the East Surrey Regiment, as passenger and to whom he was giving a joy ride, he lost one of his wheels. Captain R. Egerton went after him in a Bristol Scout (5297) to attempt to warn him. The Bristol's wheels struck the top plane of Lerwill's aircraft and the two propellers proceeded to destroy one another. This resulted in both engines

47. F. W. Lerwill in 1912, on the day that he qualified as a pilot.

accelerating until they overheated and seized up. Both machines then fell to earth from about 2,000 ft, injuring the pilots. The soldier suffered a broken arm and shock while Captain Egerton sustained concussion and a possible broken arm. Lerwill was seriously injured and had one leg amputated. Then, transferred to St Thomas's Hospital in London, he had a plate inserted into his skull and his nose rebuilt. He was flying again within a year and later commanded an RAF Station as a Major, then Squadron Leader, near to Norwich.

He was awarded the OBE on the conclusion of the war and granted a regular commission in the RAF in which he served until 1929. He next helped to superintend the development of a new aircraft, the Curlew, which was not successful. By 1937, with the prospects of war looming, Lerwill was appointed Head of ARP (Air Raid Precautions) for Barnes and Richmond. Frank Lerwill died in 1957 at the age of 76.

It is of interest to note that both his sons were educated at Eastbourne College. Godfrey, now dead, was a Brigadier, MC, in the Burma Campaign; George, his younger son, retired from the RAF as a Group Captain, DFC, and now lives in Hampshire. He has kindly provided many of the above details about his father.

1. His year of birth is often erroneously quoted as 1882.

2. The *Eastbourne Gazette* of 6 November 1912 reports that he obtained his Certificate on Sunday 3 November. This is probably the day on which he passed his test. The Certificate would be issued a few days later.

3. Gray, B. (for Capt H. E. van Goethem) in *Cross and Cockade International*, Vol 30, No 3, 1999.

Frederick Frank Minchin, born in Madras on 16 June 1890, led one of the most exotic, as well as distinguished lives of all those who learned to fly at EAC. He came of Anglo-Irish stock, the Minchins of Annagh, County Tipperary[1]. The son of a soldier, Major General F. F. Minchin, he was educated at Eastbourne College between 1905–08 where he displayed considerable sporting prowess if no prefectorial or academic achievement. Indeed his obituary in the *Old Eastbournian* in later years recorded that: 'his school

48. Freddie Minchin, *c.* 1913.

record, if not unblemished, had given evidence of what was to become one of the main features of his character', as witness a sentence from his (rugby) 'football character' in 1907: 'if a dare-devil tackle has obviously to be done, he is more than likely to do it'.

He left to enter the Royal Military College, Sandhurst, and was commissioned into the Connaught Rangers on 5 October 1910. Coming to EAC in 1912, he obtained his Certificate (No 419) on 18 February 1913 on a Bristol Boxkite. When war broke out in 1914, he was in Canada and went to France as a subaltern in Princess Patricia's Canadian Light Infantry. He soon transferred to 1 Squadron, RFC, in France and then went with 14 Squadron to the Middle East where he was awarded his first MC on 31 May 1916. The citation referred to 'conspicuous gallantry and skill on many occasions, notably when leading a successful bomb and machine-gun raid on a force of the enemy which he had located overnight. The next day he took part in two other raids. During these operations he flew for 13 hours over enemy country'.

He was awarded a bar to his MC in the *London Gazette* of 25 November 1916, the wording on this occasion being: 'He flew 150 miles at night to bomb an enemy aerodrome, descending to 500 ft and doing serious damage. On another occasion he landed 45 miles from our line to pick up the pilot of a damaged machine in hostile country'.

On 2 November 1916, while serving with 14 Squadron in Egypt and Palestine, he was in combat with enemy aircraft. The fuel tank of his Martinsyde was hit and he was forced to land near Rafa, where he burnt the aircraft. Captain R. H. Freeman, who had been escorting the damaged aircraft back to Allied lines, landed to rescue Captain Minchin, who flew back to the lines sitting on the cowl of the Martinsyde aircraft[2].

On 1 January 1917, Minchin, by now a Major, RFC, was appointed to command 47 Squadron, operating in Macedonia. He held this command until 13 March 1918, a tour of duty recognised by the award of the DSO in the *London Gazette* of 1 January 1918.

From 13 March 1918 he was based near Maidstone in Kent, commanding a wing the RAF's London Defence Area. Then on 30 March 1919, he was sent to India to command 52 Wing, engaged on frontier patrols over the Afghan border and Waziristan. He retired in March 1920 with the rank of Acting Wing Commander.

He was three times mentioned in dispatches and was also awarded the CBE. After the war he appeared to prefer to use his penultimate acting RAF rank of Lieutenant Colonel.

In 1924 Minchin joined the staff of Imperial Airways operating out of Croydon Airport where he was said to have held the speed record for a London–Paris flight. In March 1926, Minchin completed a 25,000-mile, 225-hour endurance test of a new Bristol Jupiter engine, flying a Bristol Type 84 Bloodhound between Filton and Croydon[3]. Then on 30 June he flew the Bloodhound 5,400 miles to Cairo[4] and back in 56 hours in an inaugural flight.

In September he was off again, accompanied by Major General (later Air Vice Marshall) Sir Sefton Brancker, Managing Director of Air Transport & Travel Ltd. The task was to survey the proposed airmail route to India[5]. In seven weeks they covered 3,000 miles.

29 May 1927 saw the arrival at Croydon airport of the American, Charles Lindbergh, following his solo transatlantic flight. He was escorted into Croydon by a swarm of welcoming aircraft, which included Minchin in a Handley Page Hampstead.

According to the published flight logs of Captain W. G. R. Hinchliffe, another Imperial pilot, on 27 June 1927 Minchin crash-landed the Hampstead near to Biggin Hill[6], with nine passengers aboard, due to fuel starvation in all three engines, and was dismissed [or possibly suspended] by the Company. The official accident report found him guilty of 'errors of judgement amounting to carelessness'.

It may be that this event, together with Lindbergh's achievement, inspired Minchin to undertake his last great adventure[7]. The Princess Loewenstein-Wertheim, 62, daughter of the Earl of Mexborough and a long-time aviation enthusiast, was determined to be the first woman to fly the Atlantic from east to west. She proposed to finance the venture and persuaded Minchin to be her pilot, later to be joined by Captain Leslie Hamilton, MBE, DFC, as co-pilot.

At 7.30 am on Wednesday 31 August 1927, a Fokker F VII monoplane, named the St Raphael, piloted by Minchin and heavily laden with fuel, succeeded in taking off into strong headwinds from Upavon Aerodrome, Wiltshire, destination Ottawa, Canada. The aircraft was seen

49. Minchin with the St Raphael.

passing over County Wexford, Thurles in County Tipperary and over the coast of Connemara. The steamship *Josiah Macy* reported sighting the aircraft at 9.44 pm in mid-Atlantic on the same day. No further sightings were reported and, as the aircraft's extreme flying time was 40–42 hours, it had to be assumed that it came down in the Atlantic and that the crew were lost.

50. The Minchin Memorial window and plaque.

Charles Grey, editor of *The Aeroplane*, in his obituary notice[8] on 14 September, commented that: 'Everyone liked Sq Ldr Minchin [his final RAF rank was in fact Acting Wing Commander]; he had much personal charm and a kindly nature. He was much admired for his skill and courage as a pilot. And during the war he proved himself to be a very good commanding officer. He died in the course of a great adventure in which, as those who knew him will agree, neither vanity nor the desire for gain had any part'.

His old school commemorated his life by the erection of a window and plaque in the wall of the building which overlooks Blackwater Road, Eastbourne.

1. Burke's Peerage (1904): *History of the Landed Gentry of Ireland.*

2. Henshaw, T. (1995): *The Sky their Battlefield.*

3. Stroud, J. (1962): *Annals of British and Commonwealth Air Transport 1919–1960.*

4. Higham, R. (1960): *Britain's Imperial Air Routes 1918–1939.*

5. Penrose, H. (1980): *Wings across the World: an Illustrated History of British Airways.*

6. Barnes, C. H. (1976): *Handley Page Aircraft since 1907.*

7. Barker, R. (1966): *Great Mysteries of the Air.*

8. *The Aeroplane*, 14 September 1927.

Ronald Falshaw Morkill was born on 22 November 1891 at Edinburgh, though his family must soon have moved to Bell Busk in Yorkshire.

After gaining Certificate No 535 at EAC on 1 July 1913, he served with the Canadian Engineers, the 1st Battalion of the West Yorkshire Regiment, the East Yorkshire Regiment and as a Lieutenant with 3 Reserve Squadron RFC. He was injured flying a Blériot at Shoreham on 22 June 1915 and died from his injuries the following day. At the inquest it was stated that a defect in the balance weight of a valve was discovered on examination of the wreckage after the accident.

He is buried at Kirkby Malham, Yorkshire.

51. 2/Lt R. F. Morkill in 1913.

Robert George Hamilton Murray, the son of Colonel R. D. Murray of Nevern Square, Earls Court, London, was born on 11 November 1888 in India. He entered the Royal Military College, Sandhurst, in January 1908 and was gazetted on 19 January 1909 as Second Lieutenant, Indian Army, attached 2nd Royal Highlanders.

While serving as a Lieutenant with the 9th Gurkha Rifles, he came to EAC in 1912, where he gained his RAeC Certificate No 320 on 15 October 1912.

He served in 11, 13 and 19 Squadrons with the RFC in France between October 1914 and December 1916, during which time he was

52. Lt R. G. H. Murray in 1912.

awarded the MC. He then served as a Captain in 50 Squadron based at Bekesbourne in Kent on Home Defence duties. Flying BE12s by night, he is recorded as flying on anti-Zeppelin patrols off the Kentish coast, on one occasion reaching a height of 11,000 ft. On 20 March 1917, with the rank of Major, he was appointed to command 39 Squadron at North Weald until July 1917. Intercepting a large Gotha bomber raid against Folkestone on 25 May while flying a BE12 (A6326) near the Belgian coast, he was credited with one certain and one possible kill[1]. From 22 July 1917 he commanded 31 Squadron in India, and by September 1918 was with the Egyptian Expeditionary Force, when he commanded 142 Squadron in Palestine. In addition to his MC, he was mentioned in dispatches three times (*London Gazette*: 8 May 1915, 22 June 1915 and 15 May 1917).

He was invalided to the UK in April 1919 and relinquished his commission in the October of that year.

1. Cole, C. and Cheesman, E. F. (1984): *The Air Defence of Britain 1914–1918.*

53. Lt C. H. Oxlade, RNR, in 1913.

Charles Herbert Oxlade was born at Withycombe in Somerset on 16 April 1876. Residing at Kilronan, Bexhill-on-Sea, he came to EAC as a Lieutenant in the Royal Naval Reserve and qualified on the EAC biplane with Certificate No 664 on 25 October 1913 at the age of 37. Promoted Commander, RD[1], RNR, he was killed in action when the sloop, HMS *Arbutus*, was sunk by torpedoes fired from the German submarine U 65 on Saturday 15 December 1917 in the St George's Channel, off Bristol.

His name is on the Naval Memorial on Plymouth Hoe.

1. Royal Navy Reserve Decoration.

Lambert Playfair was born on 7 December 1893 at Dibrugarh, India, the son of Harry Playfair, KCMG, a tea planter and sometime Consul General in Algiers, and his wife, Jessie. He entered the Royal Military College, Sandhurst, on a Prize Cadetship in January 1912 and was gazetted

Second Lieutenant in the 1st Battalion, The Royal Scots in January 1913. The same year he undertook flying tuition at EAC, qualifying on 11 September 1913 with Certificate No 619.

He transferred to the RFC, joining 1 Squadron in France as a pilot. Promoted Lieutenant, he was involved in combat with a 'big pusher' over Zonnebeke-Moorslede when he chased the enemy machine down to 450 ft. He was killed in action during an artillery observation patrol at 11.40 am on 6 July 1915, flying a Voisin LA (1890) with Second Lieutenant O. D. Filley, who was unhurt, in combat with two Aviatiks at 5,000 ft over St Julien[1].

54. 2/Lt Lambert Playfair in 1913.

He is buried at Hospital Farm Military Cemetery, Elverdinghe, Belgium, about four miles north-west of Ypres.

1. Henshaw, T. (1995): *The Sky their Battlefield.*

Thomas Alfred Rainey, a former Watch Officer with the Royal Mail Steam Packet Company, came to EAC as a Sub-Lieutenant, RNR. Born on 10 September 1879, his service record at the Public Record Office shows his mother living in Blackheath, London, and his wife at Southampton. Rainey passed his Certificate (No 474) on 2 May 1913 at EAC on a Bristol Boxkite in a solo flight which nearly ended in disaster. Coming into land at the airfield, he found that he was too high and so flew straight on, just skimming the roof of the Lodge Inn. Turning, he headed straight for a gasholder, missing it by two feet. On landing safely at his second attempt, he jumped down to the ground, saying to Fowler, 'How's that? I thought I was going to break up the old gasworks'. Fowler's reply has to be left to the imagination.

In mid-April, a month before qualifying, Rainey, an experienced seaman, attempted successfully to demonstrate that it was possible

55. 'Sunshine' Rainey.

to navigate with a sextant and chronometer while in flight[1]. Fowler acted as his pilot on this occasion.

In May 1913, *Flight* magazine[2] sent a reporter down to Eastbourne to research an article on the EAC. He was clearly impressed by all he saw, not least by the irrepressible Rainey, to whom he devoted almost half his article.

He wrote, 'If anyone could be in the company of Mr Rainey for ten minutes without feeling it is good to be alive, he must be in a bad way'. This view is perhaps confirmed by his nickname at the time: 'Sunshine Rainey'.

Appointed Flight Sub-Lieutenant on 1 October 1913, Rainey served with 3 Squadron at the Isle of Grain RNAS station through much of 1914. He appears to have had a certain proneness to accidents, crashing a Bristol TB8 biplane at Leigh-on-Sea in February and then on 4 May 1914, when flying from Shoreham in a RNAS two-seater Sopwith tractor biplane (Serial No 27), he landed with engine trouble in a field near the Sussex Pad hotel on the A27 Brighton–Worthing road. After his mechanic, who was travelling with him, attended to the engine, he took off again. This time, he had got a few feet into the air when the engine failed again and the aircraft turned over. The mechanic leapt clear but Rainey was severely shaken[3]. He later severely damaged another Bristol at St Margaret's Bay in September[4].

56. Rainey's crash at Shoreham, May 1914, with the Sussex Pad in the background.

By the end of 1914, Rainey, now a Flight Lieutenant, RNAS, was a member of Commander C. R. Samson's Eastchurch Squadron, based at Dunkirk. Their remit included patrolling against enemy aircraft and Zeppelins and general reconnaissance. On 29 September 1914, Rainey and four others were sent to Lille in Bristol TB8 biplanes. On the way Rainey had to force-land, due to engine failure, in an area between Dunkirk and Lille where there was fighting between Belgian and German troops. According to Commander Samson's record[5], Rainey 'spent a lively two or three minutes dodging an Uhlan round and round his aeroplane, having unfortunately left his pistol in his seat; luckily, just as the situation was getting rather too exciting even for Rainey, some Belgian cyclists arrived and dealt with this Uhlan. The aeroplane had to be burnt, as a large body of Germans appeared'.

On another occasion, Rainey returned from a bombing raid in a Maurice Farman. Again according to Commander Samson: 'Rainey approached the aerodrome flying very low, and proceeded to give us an exhibition of his skill in handling the big aeroplane; most of us were out on the aerodrome watching him, as although he was a very determined pilot he was not always very skilful in his landings'. Interest in his manoeuvres was quickly spoilt when one of the observers exclaimed: 'Good Lord, sir, he has got a bomb hanging on his chassis wires'. His observers quickly bolted for cover, expecting every minute that the bomb would drop off. They signalled to him to try to attract his attention to the bomb, but he didn't understand their frantic wavings and kept on circling over the hangar in which they were sheltering. Eventually he landed, and came taxi-ing towards the hangar at full speed. The bomb hung on, although only caught up by one of its fan blades. Rainey did not get a good reception!

On 1 October 1914[6], Rainey was piloting a Bristol TB8 (916) when his fuel tank was shot up, causing him to crash-land. The aircraft proved unsalvable.

On 17 December 1914, Rainey, flying a Maurice Farman Biplane (1240) of 2 Naval Aeroplane Squadron on a mission to bomb the submarine depot at Bruges, was forced by shelling to crash-land at Breskens in Holland[7]. His aircraft was damaged beyond repair and Rainey was interned in Holland. As Commander Samson commented:

'I was not too downcast over his absence, as I felt certain he would turn up sooner or later, as he was such a redoubtable fellow, competent to get out of any trouble'. He later escaped to England by stowing away in the coal bunker of a ship. He was promoted Flight Commander on 25 June 1915 and posted to Mesopotamia in February 1916. Subsequently in March 1916 he was attached to 2 Wing at Thasos in the northern Aegean. In January 1917 was sent to Cranwell to 're-qualify', then to 3 Wing, classified as 'sick'. He was invalided from the Service on 17 September 1917.

1. *Flight,* 26 April 1913.

2. *Flight,* 10 May 1913.

3. & 4. Sturtevant, R. and Page, G. (1992): *Royal Naval Aircraft Serials and Units 1911–1919.*

5. Samson, C. R. (1930): *Fights and Flights.*

6. Henshaw, T. (1995): *The Sky their Battlefield.*

7. van Dorssen, H. and Gerdessen, F. in *Cross and Cockade Great Britain,* Vol 16, No 1, 1985.

57. W. S. Roberts in 1913.

William Sterling Roberts, born at Lewisham on 7 May 1878, passed his test with Certificate No 558 at Eastbourne on the EAC Boxkite on 3 July 1913 at the age of 35, while lodging at Stone Wall Gardens, Stone Cross. Nothing has been discovered of his subsequent career.

Arthur Ashford Benjamin Thomson, popularly known as Ack Ack Beer, was born at Dinapore, India, on 2 April 1895 and educated at Wellington College 1907–11. He learnt to fly at EAC, while lodging at 36 Cavendish Place. He qualified on 1 April 1913 with Certificate No 452. The same year he was gazetted Second Lieutenant in the RFC (Special Reserve) and the following year received a permanent commission with the Royal Warwickshire Regiment, seconded to the RFC. After a course at the Central Flying School at Upavon, he served with 1 and 16 Squadrons in France from 1914–16. In the early days of the war he was known for flying low over the German trenches and firing at their troops with a rifle or automatic pistol, the only armament at the time. On 21 September 1915, near Armentières, he shot up and damaged an enemy Albatros which he pursued as far as Wytschaete. He was awarded the MC on 2 October 1915 'For conspicuous gallantry and determination on August 29 1915, near Neuve Chapelle. When ranging a heavy gun on the German trenches he stayed up over two hours in heavy rain, with clouds at about 500 ft. At one time he found himself in a cloud on the far side of the German trenches; but, after coming back under heavy fire, he continued to observe with the greatest bravery and skill, only returning when too dark for more work. His gallant conduct resulted in 10 direct hits on the enemy's parapet'.

58. A. A. B. Thomson as Air Commodore, c. 1938.

He served in 15, 33 and 50 Squadrons in Home Defence in Yorkshire and Kent from 1916 to 1918. In 1916 he received a bar to his MC for good work on anti-Zeppelin patrols. During the night of 24/25 September 1917, while commanding 33 Squadron, Major Thomson flew three anti-Zeppelin sorties in a FE2d (B1885), spending no less than four and a quarter hours in the air, confirming his reputation as one of the most energetic of home defence COs[1]. In the same year, aged 22, he became Wing Commander, acting Lieutenant Colonel. He was mentioned in dispatches and was awarded the AFC in 1918.

After the war, he obtained a permanent commission in the RAF, specialising in armament duties. Between 1920 and 1927, he served in missions to Austria and Hungary and at HQ Iraq. From 1930–33, he was Assistant Director (Armaments) at the Air Ministry. By 1938 he was promoted Air Commodore, the youngest officer of this rank, and given command of No 3 Bomber Group. On 28 August 1939 he was fatally injured at RAF, Boscombe Down, after backing into an idling propeller following a test flight in a Wellington. He died on his way to hospital.

1. Cole, C. and Cheesman, E. F. (1984): *The Air Defence of Britain 1914–1918.*

John Edmund Burnet Thornely was born on 5 July 1896 at Cambridge. Another pilot to qualify at Eastbourne, 'Steve' Thornely, the son of a Cambridge University professor, of Merton Hall, passed his test at 17 years of age, but had to wait until the legal qualifying age for aviators before gaining Certificate No 831 on his 18th birthday on 5 July 1914.

59. 'Steve' Thornely in 1914.

Thornely is best remembered for an escapade which may have made aviation history. While Fowler and Hucks were at the 1914 Olympia Aero Show, in London, young Thornely, on 23 March, took off in a Henry Farman biplane, strengthened with extra wires to Gassler's design. He climbed to 3,500 ft before diving to loop-the-loop. Thornely is thought to be the youngest pilot to perform this manoeuvre and this was believed to be the first occasion on which it was achieved by a biplane. The novelty did not save Thornely from the wrath of Fowler and Hucks on their return from London. Looping-the-loop was at that time held to be the prerogative of Gustav Hamel and B. C. Hucks, and intrusion upon their glory was apparently unwelcome.

Thornely's father had hired and later purchased an EAC-built Maurice Farman for his son's exclusive use. In May 1914, Thornely, with Fowler's approval, took this Maurice Farman to Germany to give displays of looping. He visited Mannheim on 17 May, Frankfurt on 18/19 and Munster on the 21st. He was accompanied by two mechanics, Will

60. Thornely in the Farman at Munster, 1914.

Dowsett and Ernie Palethorpe, both from EAC, and was planning to go on to Pforzheim, Hamburg, Bremen and Hanover. Unfortunately the displays came to an end when the aircraft was damaged in a crash at Munster. Thornely was not injured and all three returned to Eastbourne.

61. The crashed Farman at Munster.

We are indebted to the late Mr Trevor Dowsett, son of Will Dowsett, for the use of two photographs of Thornely's visit to Germany. One, showing the wrecked machine, was sent as a postcard on 28 May to Miss Bessie Love, the future Mrs Dowsett, at 3 Cricketfield Cottage, Ashford Road, Eastbourne. It bears the laconic inscription: 'How do you like this for a smash – he managed to do it properly'. Many years later, in 1973, Mrs Dowsett, referring to her late husband, told Michael Goodall: 'he loved every hour that he spent with the EAC. It was a sad day for us when they folded up'.

Thornely, like many young men of his age, volunteered for military service and was appointed Flight Sub-Lieutenant, RNAS, on 5 August 1914 and posted to Eastchurch for advanced flying training.

It seems probable that he was either interned in Holland or a prisoner of war, because his records show that he was repatriated in October 1915, having been recommended for a mention in dispatches on 14 June 1915, though with no supporting information. During 1916 he served with 49 and 27 Squadrons and in December was admitted to hospital and assigned to light duties. By August 1917, he held a staff appointment at the War Office.

He subsequently reached the rank of Major, RFC/Squadron Leader, RAF, and was awarded the OBE in the New Year Honours List of 1 January 1919.

He left the RAF on 20 June 1918 on account of ill-health, but was allowed to retain his rank.

62. Pilots and airfield staff, 1913. *Back row:* Victor Yates, unknown, unknown, unknown, unknown, Rueben Marsh, unknown, Dick Laker, unknown, unknown, Ernie Palethorpe, Jack Barrow. *Front row:* Frank Hucks, 'Steve' Thornely, 'Brian' Hunt, unknown, F. B. Fowler, Emil Gassler, Cyril Foggin?, Will Dowsett, unknown.

71

The First World War

The original thoughts which accompanied the new science of flying had many variations. In the local Press on 11 March 1914 one reads that Fowler was joining in the activities of the Hailsham Harriers by trailing the course of the hare from his aeroplane, thus giving the most accurate clues as to the line to follow. A 1914 directory, *Who's Who in Aviation*, lists Fowler's recreations as tennis, shooting and yachting with his clubs the Royal Aero, Sussex Motor Yacht and the Devonshire Club of Eastbourne.

With prospects of war looming, Emil Gassler decided to return to Switzerland where he was rejected for service in the Swiss Air Corps. The next year he joined Luft Verkehrs Gesellschaft (LVG), a German aircraft manufacturer, as a test pilot and instructor at Johannisthal Aerodrome, near Berlin. In 1917 he moved to Border Aeroplane Repair Works of Golm, Potsdam, working on Rumpler C biplanes. It has been suggested that Gassler was later involved in the formation of the Swiss national airline, Swissair.

It was clearly the possibility of war that led the Admiralty to contribute to the costs of one of the EAC seaplane hangars on the Crumbles for use as a fuel depot and repair workshop.

The entire story changed – as it changed for millions of other people – with the outbreak of the Great War on 4 August 1914. Life was never to be the same again, for Fowler, or for anyone else.

CONTRACTORS TO THE ADMIRALTY.

EASTBOURNE
AVIATION Co. LTD.

AEROPLANE BUILDERS.

TELEPHONE—1176.   TELEGRAMS—"1176 EASTBOURNE."

63. An EAC advertisement, 1914–1915.

On the outbreak of war, the EAC Airfield was taken over by the Admiralty, in the form of the Royal Naval Air Service (RNAS), as a training station. Another two hangars were added at the north end of the lane that is now known as Leeds Avenue. The Admiralty also, by 1917, erected 15 Bessoneau hangars for aircraft storage, nine alongside Lottbridge Drove and six adjacent to Leeds Avenue. These were pre-fabricated wood and canvas structures measuring 20×24 metres, each holding between three and six machines.

Civilian use of the airfield was stopped on 5 August 1914. This was perhaps unfortunate for Fowler and EAC, as other training schools such as the Beatty, Ruffy Baumann, Hall

S.—1502. (Established—Nov., 1913.)

PASS

FOR

Entry into R.N.A.S. Eastbourne

Date of Issue _____

Nature of Pass _____

Number of Pass _____

This Certificate enables the bearer—

Name in full _____

Address _____

Business _____
    to pass into the _____
    on the business above declared.
Date of expiration of pass *May 12ᵗʰ 1918*

64. An Entry Pass to the RNAS Aerodrome.

and Grahame-White Schools at Hendon continued to operate throughout the war. However, Fowler continued in charge until 1 February 1915;

65. F. B. Fowler with the first batch of RNAS pupils, October 1914.
Back row: **Probationary Flight Sub-Lieuts B. L. Huskisson, M. E. A. Wright, V. Nicholl, D. Iron.**
Seated: **Prob Flight Sub-Lieut J. J. Petre, F. B. Fowler, Chief Instructor, Mr Hardstaff, Assistant Instructor, Prob Flight Sub-Lieut F. G. T. Dawson.**

indeed on 21 October 1914, *The Aeroplane* featured a photograph on its front cover of him sitting amidst his first batch of six RNAS pupils. One of this batch was Flight Sub-Lieutenant (later Air Commodore) Douglas Iron. In an article[1] in 1975, he commented that 'Our three Boxkites had neither dual control nor instruments of any kind . . . ailerons were still of the single acting variety, and hung down until sufficient speed had been gained over the ground to make them operate; and the rotary engine had no means to throttle it down to reduce its revolutions. It was a matter of full out or stop, until one got the hang of it. Nevertheless, in spite of this somewhat dicey state of affairs, we all passed out and received the Royal Aero Club Certificate, known as the ticket, after a comparatively short time in the air'.

Further land was leased by the navy from the Duke of Devonshire and added to the approximate 50 acres of Fowler's original airfield. By 1918 RAF records show that the airfield was 242 acres in extent. The Seaplane Base, which remained in EAC hands throughout the war, was much smaller, as can be seen in the map at Appendix 1. The RNAS closed the Eastbourne base temporarily on 9 November 1916, transferring it, according to some accounts, to Vendôme in France. The airfield remained under the sole supervision of Sub-Lieutenant R. Spickernell, RNVR, until it reopened under Squadron Commander Murphy on 13 April 1917.

Security seems to have been handled differently in this war, as newspaper reports appeared periodically throughout the period of the conflict. For example, on 20 January 1915, *The Aeroplane* reported on damage done to the aerodrome by gales. Apparently sheds nos 1, 2 and 3 were blown down and three Boxkites and a brand new Maurice Farman were in the wreck. The article goes on to say that the workshops stood up to the wind and in any case were being moved shortly to the seaplane station; flying training for the Probationary Flight Sub-Lieutenants was disrupted and they were kept busy with other branches of their training. It also remarked that Mr Fowler was last Tuesday and Wednesday at Hendon putting a new Henry Farman through its tests for the Admiralty.

The Aeroplane of 23 June 1915 reported on a collision on the seafront between an Eastbourne taxi-cab and an RNAS motor vehicle, which sadly resulted in the death of the taxi-cab driver, Ernest Henry Chinnery. The RNAS vehicle was being driven on the wrong side of the road, and

66. A staff group at the Seaplane Base, c. 1915. Mr C. Smith in centre, Dolly Parker (*née* Morris) on far left, Max Ford on ground, far right, Will Dowsett 3rd from left, standing.

the article comments that when driving in the dark with compulsory dim lights it is the safest thing to do! 'The only way to be sure of missing pedestrians, cyclists and barrows is to drive slightly to the right of the crown of the road.'

The first fatal flying accident of the period took place on 10 March 1915 and unfortunately such events continued at intervals until the day before the war ended. A record of the fatalities which occurred at and around the airfield is included later in this chapter.

Less serious incidents were also reported in the local Press from time to time:

Aviator's Fall
Serious Accident at Eastbourne

About half past five yesterday morning an accident occurred to an aviator at Eastbourne. The weather was fine and bright and the conditions in regard to wind were also favourable. It is stated that the aviator made an ascent and had to alight owing to engine trouble, and that on going up again he fell with the machine. The crash was so loud that some of the occupants of houses in the vicinity were awakened and rose to see what had happened. Assistance was at once rendered to the aviator, who appeared to be badly hurt and was removed to the Kempston Red Cross Hospital[2]. The accident was at first regarded as a very serious one; but we were glad to learn last night that although the aviator, Lieutenant L. C. Keeble, was very severely shaken he is going on so well that his speedy recovery is hoped for.

Eastbourne Gazette, 2 June 1915.

And again:

Aviator in a Pond
Praiseworthy Action of Civilians

Another flying accident, which, happily, was not attended by fatal consequences, occurred on the Crumbles on Sunday, when an unfortunate aviator was rescued from a pond by a number of civilians. Squadron Commander F. B. Fowler, the commanding officer of the RNAS at Eastbourne, writes concerning this:

'I should be extremely obliged if you would, through the medium of your paper, express my sincerest thanks to all the men who, on Sunday last, rendered such prompt assistance in an aeroplane accident. The machine involved fell into the Crumbles pond, and a number of men, in spite of the fact that they were in their Sunday clothes, dashed through some two ft of mud and water, to the assistance of the unfortunate pilot. It is considered that their action under the circumstances was most praiseworthy, and I hope this letter will be seen by them all, so that they may know how it was appreciated'.

Eastbourne Gazette, 30 January 1918.

And yet again:

Boy injured by Aeroplane

Yesterday (Tuesday) morning a boy named Kitcher, of Winkney Cottages, Hampden Park, was walking alongside a hedge in a field when he was struck by an aeroplane which crashed through the hedge. The aeroplane had apparently made a false landing. Kitcher, who was rendered unconscious, was conveyed to the Princess Alice Memorial Hospital.

Eastbourne Gazette, 30 October 1918.

Fowler's War Service*

Fowler continued to run the training station in a civilian capacity until Squadron Commander Shepherd was appointed Commanding Officer on 1 February 1915, on which date Fowler was granted a temporary commission as Flight Lieutenant, RNAS. (Details of commanding officers during the war years are given at Appendix 10. RNAS ranks and their equivalents in the other services are detailed at Appendix 11.) His first posting was to the Isle of Grain on 29 March 1915 and he remained there or at nearby Eastchurch until 4 December 1915 when he was posted to the Central Flying School at Upavon, Wiltshire, for advanced flying instruction. He was promoted temporary Flight Commander on 30 June 1916, and temporary Squadron Commander on 30 June 1917. Then on 24 January 1916 he was back to the Isle of Grain, said to be the first seaplane base in Britain and from where he flew on anti-submarine patrols. It was so remote that even by 1920 it was not on the public telephone system. Ashworth[3] records that 2 Squadron, RNAS, (later designated 2 Wing), was transferred from Grain to Dunkirk, near Calais, in August 1915 and this may explain why we find reference to Fowler flying from there, though there is no evidence of such a posting in his records at the Public Record Office (PRO). On one occasion while flying on an anti-submarine patrol mission over the Channel, he spotted a German Zeppelin low down on the water. Turning into the attack, he dived on the giant shape below and was just about to release his bombs when he spotted a British destroyer alongside. It had been hidden from view by the enormous bulk of the envelope until the crucial moment.

On 5 May 1916 he moved to Cranwell as senior flying instructor. In April 1917 he returned to RNAS, Eastbourne, and on 31 October 1917 was appointed Commanding Officer of his own airfield, responsible for training on Avro 504Ks and Sopwith Camels. He had a number of the Camels converted to two-seater specification in an attempt to protect trainees from their handling difficulties.

In 1918, after further advanced training, he moved to 3 TDS (Training Depot Station) at Lopcombe Corner, near to Andover in Hampshire and then in November to 43 TDS at Chattis Hill, near to Stockbridge, Hampshire. Altogether, Fowler flew some 2,000 hours during the war.

(*See Appendix 12.)

HMS *Vindex*

It has frequently been suggested that Fowler was the first, or certainly one of the first, to fly a landplane from the deck of a Royal Navy vessel. (As stated earlier, Commander Samson had previously performed this feat.) However, it is a fact that on 3 November 1915 a Bristol Scout (1255) took off from the deck of HMS *Vindex*, a converted Isle of Man passenger steamer. Sturtivant and Page[4], and Layman[5], are clear that the pilot was Fowler. Roskill[6], though recording the pilot as B. F. Fowler, states that Jones and Raleigh[7] give him as H. F. Towler. Burns and Nailer[8],

67. HMS *Vindex*, the converted Isle of Man ferry, SS *Viking*.

in an article in *Cross and Cockade International* (Vol 17, No 3, 1986) state that 'there can be no doubt that the pilot . . . was Fowler', as he is named several times in the Admiralty report (Adm. 1/8432/253). However, they note that someone has defaced Fowler's name on page 14 and substituted that of Towler.

The *Vindex*, formerly the SS *Viking*, operated in peacetime on the Fleetwood–Douglas run and continued to do so until the 1930s when returned to her owners. A flying deck of 64 ft long and 28 ft in width (narrowing to 8 ft aft) was constructed, and in operation the vessel was capable of housing up to nine aircraft.

Burns and Nailer state that two Bristol Scouts (1246 and

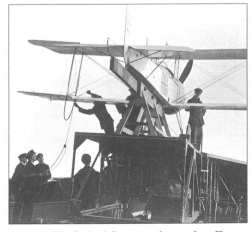

68. The Bristol Scout ready to take off from *Vindex*.

79

69. Fowler taking off from *Vindex*.

1255) were employed on the test flights and that the pilot was Flight Commander Fowler[9] for all experiments. A photograph shows Bristol Scout 1255 prepared for flight with 'the tail guide trestle mounted on the retractable deck section and the tail skid in place on the guide'. This is important in that Sturtivant and Page record that on 7 October 1915 Flight Commander[9] B. F. Fowler tested the tail guide trestle strop, flying from Eastchurch. They go on to record that on 3 November 1915 Fowler, piloting Bristol Scout 1255, became the first man to launch a landplane from the deck of a naval vessel, HMS *Vindex*, specifically equipped for the purpose. This was in the vicinity of the *Mouse* light vessel, in the Thames estuary (51°31'N, 00°58'E). Fowler flew on to land at Eastchurch.

It may be worth commenting that this was a hazardous and brave experiment which had on previous occasions resulted in the loss of the pilot's life.

Mr Tapp's Memories

Caffyns Ltd, the Eastbourne-based motor company, was also involved in aircraft production during the war, as the next few paragraphs explain.

Their work was recalled by the late Mr Leslie Tapp of Meadow Place, Westham, near Eastbourne, who worked for them in 1914–18, and later as an electrician in their motor business. He remembered the details thus:

**70. Nellie Hart (centre), forewoman, with staff
from the fabric sewing room.**

'At Caffyns motor works in Marine Parade, during the war, seventy-five SE5a Scout aeroplanes were built[10]. They were designed by the Royal Aircraft Factory at Farnborough, but made or assembled by many different firms throughout the country'. Mr Tapp continued 'They were first fitted with Hispano Suiza 150 hp engines which were 90 degree V8 water cooled; in, I think, 1918, they were succeeded by 200 hp Wolseley Viper engines. The wing-span of the 'planes was 26 ft 7½ inches, the wing-length 12 ft and the wing-width 5 ft; the main spar of the box section, made of spruce, carried the aileron hinges. The ribs were of spruce strips and bars, no plywood being used, and on the main spar a double pulley-bracket was fitted to carry the control cables. The wings were covered with best quality unbleached linen sewn together with thin string. The joins were covered with strips of linen cut from spaced fabric, with a side fringe to improve adhesion when stuck on with a special dope-glue. The string was then sewn right through both surfaces of the wing to prevent the fabric coming away from the wing frame. Wings were then doped on both sides, dried slowly in a warm workshop, then varnish-waterproofed and painted'.

Mr Tapp continued 'Three different types of dope[11] were used, namely Emallite, Cellon, and Titanine. The centre-sections of the wings were strongly made and covered with plywood to allow the mounting of a gun. The tail-skid contained two large compression springs to take the tail-weight on landing, and a laminated skid-shoe to steer the aircraft on the ground. The aileron hinges were stamped from Lysaght's 14-gauge aviation steel, and the tubing for body-struts and other parts was made by Accles & Pollock. The "joy-sticks" or control columns were made from $1\frac{1}{8}$ inch outside diameter brass tubing. A universal joint was fitted about two-thirds of the way down, with a fitting at the lower end to take the cables to ailerons and elevators. Wing-spar brackets were built from steel plates, for attaching the wings to the fuselage. Rudder bars were made of 9-plywood covered with 22-gauge aluminium, and fitted with a delta metal brush'.

Another of Mr Tapp's memories tells us something of Fowler's character and courage: 'Two riggers who were used to working together assembling 'planes, mostly Maurice Farmans, at the RNAS Aerodrome, had a certain amount of spare time on their hands. So one day they asked Commander Fowler if he would let them build a Farman from scrap parts taken from various crashes. He gave them permission to do so, saying it would be good practice for them.

They worked hard on this for weeks, taking a good wing from one crashed 'plane, a tail from another, then a good nacelle [the body enclosing the crew and engine] from yet another and overhauling an engine and so on until at last they had completely assembled a machine, the qualities of which were unknown. They checked and rechecked all the controls and the engine, to satisfy themselves that the 'plane was, in their opinion, airworthy. There was only one thing they could not do, however, and that was to try it out. It needed a pilot to do that, and what pilot would risk his life flying a kite built out of scrap? They went to Commander Fowler and told him that they had finished it and asked him if he would come and inspect it. He said he was busy, but he would have a look at it when he had the time. The great moment came when he walked over to the machine and asked the riggers, "So you think it will fly, do you?". One of them said, "Well sir, we've checked everything, and to our knowledge it seems to be OK". Commander Fowler replied, "All right then, I'll take it up". One of the riggers, who had done most of the work on it, asked if he could be a passenger in the observer's seat, to which request Commander Fowler's answer was quite emphatic, "No, certainly not, only one man is going to risk his life in this".

He made a perfect take-off and flew away from the watchers. He was a long time gone and the two riggers awaited anxiously. At last he was seen coming back, he circled the 'drome and made a perfect landing. He got out of the 'plane and walked towards the two men. They wondered what he was going to say about the 'plane, as he was a very particular man, and was always criticising the work done in the workshops. They anticipated that he would say that the 'plane was "heavy on the controls", "swinging to the left or right", or that "it was a rough engine". Instead, he congratulated the two men on their splendid work, and said that this machine was the finest Maurice Farman he had ever flown, and that it was even better than some of the new ones previously delivered at the aerodrome'.

Mr Tapp also recalled the Avro 504 trainers which used to arrive from the manufacturers at Eastbourne station and which were then towed through the town by Crossley trucks to the airfield where they would be assembled. Their rotary engines, he recalled, used to give a certain amount of ignition trouble. The aircraft would land wherever they could and the pilot or trainee would clean the commutator with a rag soaked in petrol. 'One day an Avro came down in a field near the railway station [at Westham] with this trouble and Arthur "Boy" Chaston and I went over to it and helped the take-off by holding onto the wing struts while the engine was revved; then we let go when the pilot raised his hand.'

EAC during the War

By 18 March 1915, an American, Edward Mayo Chapman of 9 Milnthorpe Road, Eastbourne, had become a Director. The registered office of the EAC was changed in February 1916 to the Seaplane Base on the Crumbles. During the war years, 12 BE2cs, 40 Maurice Farman S11s, 200 (possibly only 150) Avro 504Ls and six Avro 504Ks (see

71. EAC group with a BE2c at the Seaplane Base, 1915. Frank Hucks centre, Dick Laker sitting third from left.

Appendix 3) were built by EAC at the Seaplane Base, which also undertook much repair work on military aircraft. There can be little doubt of the standing of the EAC at this time, for on 16 June 1916 the Company was elected a full member of the Society of British Aircraft Constructors. Membership was proposed by Mr G. Holt Thomas, Chief Executive of the Aircraft Manufacturing Company Limited, one of the most illustrious names in pioneer aviation. Charles Smith, of 62 Belmore Road, Eastbourne, was shown as Secretary (in place of Hucks who, as stated earlier, was on active service in the Royal Navy) and General Manager.

The RNAS in Eastbourne

We have identified records of 117 RNAS pilots who qualified for their certificates at the Eastbourne Station (see Appendix 13); these included a number from the Dominions and at least eighteen from Canada. In addition, nine Brazilian and an unknown number of American and Japanese pilots were trained at Eastbourne. In the early years the RNAS Officers Mess for Eastbourne Airfield was in the town at Eversley Court[12], 14 St Anne's Road, and the officers travelled to and from the airfield in a large charabanc. This property was purchased by Eastbourne Corporation in the early 1920s and became the Boys' Municipal School, later renamed the Grammar School. It remains basically the same, with some additions, and is now, in 1999, a part of the Eastbourne College of Arts & Technology. Later a number of private schools in the town, such as South Lynn, Aldro, Ascham St Vincent's and Hill Brow were utilised. Redmont, a large private house in Trinity Place, was also converted into a mess. It was reported in the *Eastbourne Gazette* of 26 July 1916 that the licensee of the Lodge Inn, Seaside, Mr Theodore Frederick Barrett, provided a canteen for airfield personnel and billeted thirty men. Teas were provided for officers in the spring and autumn. What happened in the summer and winter was not reported!

One of the second batch of RNAS trainees was Probationary Flight Sub-Lieutenant A. H. Sandwell, who was posted to Eastbourne in May 1915. His experiences were recorded in *Cross and Cockade Great Britain Journal*[13] in 1982 and we give here an extract which gives a flavour of life there in 1915:

'The RNAS flying school at Eastbourne was run on humane and commonsense lines, in contradistinction to some camps of which I have been told. Its skipper, Squadron Commander Shepherd, was a "pukka NO" (a genuine Naval Officer) who had seen service afloat in the Persian Gulf and who could swear in five or six languages, including Arabic and Hindustani. With one exception, F/Lt R. Hilton Jones, the instructors had themselves learned to fly not more than six weeks previously.

The small aerodrome was not only surrounded by dykes (ditches in this part of England), but was bisected by one which was partially bridged over. The machines were of heterogeneous origin and were there either because they were unsuitable for war service or had been retired on account of old age and/or obsolescence. In the latter category was 873, an 80-Gnome Avro [504] which had taken part in the raid on the Dusseldorf [actually Friedrichshafen] Zeppelin sheds. There was a Short [S38] pusher with visiting-card elevators in front, on which I had my first tuition. Its official number was 28. A similar machine numbered 3 had at least been rebuilt. Heaven knows how many pilots had learned to fly (if it *was* flying?) on these machines.

After exactly 68 minutes dual and a 43 minute flip in an Avro, I was pushed off solo on the Short. On my first landing I found that I was trundling directly towards an unbridged part of the dyke, so took off again and next time in avoiding the central dyke, I overshot and pulled up miraculously intact ten or 15 ft from the boundary ditch. The first thing I heard was the skipper's voice booming across the field, accusing me of the one form of moral turpitude of which I am physiologically incapable. "If he calls me that for not running into a ditch" I thought, "what would he have said if I had crashed?" But after mess that night he told me I was doing well, and thenceforth I would have gone to hell for him.

Before there was much chance of getting in many more hours – or minutes – on 28, she was crashed by another pupil, so I switched to tractors in the shape of 80 hp Gnome Caudrons. It was on one of these that I did my ticket flights on 16 June 1915. Thereafter I flipped Avros and a White and Thompson, and on one of the former carried my first passenger when I had amassed 7 hours 42 minutes flying time.

Some rather moth-eaten, or rather rat-eaten, Blériot monoplanes arrived about then. Without any dual whatever, some of us were shoved onto these rather extraordinary machines, and the very next day I was sent cross-country on one of them to visit the RFC camp at Shoreham.

My introduction to the Corps which I had almost joined in 1913 was hardly propitious. My magneto switch was faulty, the 80 Gnome refused to switch off, and after running and bouncing the full length of the aerodrome, we finally came to rest with the Blériot and a Maurice Farman Longhorn in a death clinch. "Was the Major rude to you?" asked my CO when I reported to him by telephone. "Not a bit, he was speechless!"

Next day the skipper told me I was appointed to Dundee for duty. "I think they have seaplanes there!" he said. I didn't care. I had 10 hours 47 minutes – on land machines'.

The only recorded operational sortie[14] flown from the RNAS airfield took place on 25 April 1916 when, at 0425 hours, three aircraft took off to patrol the channel. The machines involved were a Bristol Scout C (3060) piloted by Flight Lieutenant M. S. Marsden, an EAC-built BE2c (1183) flown by Flight Lieutenant L. A. Jones and Flight Sub-Lieutenant A. Durstan and a Maurice Farman S11 (1846) flown by Flight Sub-Lieutenants W. G. McMinnies and F. W. Walker. The first aircraft force-landed at Lympne, while the other two returned to Eastbourne about one and a half hours later. The patrol was officially listed as a home defence sortie, probably an anti-Zeppelin patrol, although the records are not clear on this point.

Wing Commander E. D. Crundall, DFC, recalls in his memoirs[15] his time at RNAS Eastbourne in the autumn of 1916, which had its lighter moments: 'All officers were billeted in nice houses in the town. One of my room-mates had on occasions tried to attract the attention of a young lady in a window opposite to our billet. After many days without encouragement he signalled to her in morse code with a hairbrush. She picked up something and signalled back, telling him she was a Girl Guide and her mother was very strict, so she could never

72. E. D. Crundall in 1916.

meet or speak to him openly'. Crundall also recollects a fellow pupil, 'rather dim in mentality', who recorded in his log book: 'Most curious, saw birds flying backwards'. Another pupil, on his first solo on a Maurice Farman, came in too high to land. 'He pushed the machine down until the wheels struck the ground and the machine bounced clean over a hangar. Luckily he had the sense to open up the engine and fly away correctly. Next time he made a smooth landing but the previous bounce had broken all his landing wires in the wings. As the machine ran along the ground, gradually losing momentum, the wings slowly collapsed and trailed along the ground, rather like a tired bird. Then, quite slowly, the undercarriage began to collapse and the machine did a waltz-like twist to one side, and the unfortunate pupil found himself sitting on the ground'.

Throughout the war, the social side of life continued for the RNAS personnel. Football matches were played against the RAMC Camp at Summerdown, Eastbourne Gas Company, Polegate Airship Station, Eastbourne Aviation Company and other local teams. There were no records of cricket matches. Children's Christmas parties were arranged in the various messes and successful charity concerts were also performed by airfield personnel, known as the 'Flyghties', at locations such as the Town Hall and the Central Wesleyan Church in Langney Road.

The Travers Diaries

Herbert Gardner Travers, who was born in 1891 and known within his family as 'H', was another who learned to fly with the RNAS at Eastbourne. He had served in France with the HAC (Honourable Artillery Company), a territorial unit, from September 1914 until he sustained a severe wound to his right hand and arm in December of that year. He then underwent painful treatment in various hospitals in England while his wound was cleaned and healed. He had already begun flying lessons at the Beatty School at Hendon before the war and so, as soon as he was fit, he applied for and was granted a temporary commission as a Probationary Flight Sub-Lieutenant in the RNAS, exactly one year after he had been wounded. On 4 January 1916, he was posted to RNAS, Eastbourne, where his brother Jim had in 1912 piloted one of the Henry Farman seaplanes in the 'Wake up England' tour.

We owe it to his daughter, Miss Eva Travers, that we have a record of his ten or so weeks at Eastbourne. Her book[16], which describes the lives of the three Travers brothers, all notable aviators, and from which she has generously allowed us to quote, uses H's log books and his letters to his family to compile a uniquely factual account of his training, the aircraft in which he flew and the pilots with whom he flew (Appendix 14 contains a verbatim record). He qualified after 64 minutes solo! He went on to a distinguished war record, first in France where he was involved in 25 combats with enemy

73. H. G. Travers in 1916.

aircraft (accounting for five) and later, as acting Squadron Commander, then Major, DSC, commanding 11 Squadron, RNAS/211 Squadron, RAF, before he was posted to Home Establishment in England.

Capital Reconstruction

Despite the intensive activity on the manufacturing side during the war years, there is some evidence that all was not well financially. By virtue of a Special Resolution of the Company, the High Court on 22 March 1917 and 10 April 1917 approved a reduction of the Authorised Share Capital to £10,500. This was now made up of 5,000 Ordinary Shares of 14/- [70p] and 10,000 Preference Shares, also of 14/-. Of these, 3,247 of the ordinary shares had been issued as well as the whole of the preference shares. A reduction of capital of this nature is usually a sign that a company has been trading unprofitably and that the shareholders have been persuaded to accept a reduction in the nominal and also the real value of their investment.

The RAF Survey of 1918

On 1 April 1918, the hitherto separate RNAS and RFC were amalgamated into one military air service, the Royal Air Force (RAF). So Eastbourne became for a short while an RAF Training Depot Station.

It may be worth noting the particulars recorded in the official *RAF Survey* of 1 November 1918 (see Appendix 15). The population of

Eastbourne at that time was said to be 52,500; the nearest railway station was Eastbourne on the London, Brighton and South Coast Railway, and there is mention of a railway siding near the airfield, known locally as the ballast line.

Eastbourne Airfield is quoted as having maximum dimensions of 2,000 yards by 1,000 yards, covering 242 acres, of which 10 acres were covered by station buildings. The height is given as 15 ft above sea level, and there is a reminder that 'some of the sewers are covered, but some are not'. The Station was in the 60th Wing of the RAF, part of No 2 Group, in the South-East Area. Described on 15 July 1918 as No 50 TDS, it had three units of single-seater fighters on which to train, comprising 36 Camels and 36 Avros[17]. There were 171 officers (of whom 120 were in training) 216 women, not including hostel staff employed away from the airfield, and 452 Warrant Officers, NCOs and airmen, making a total of 839. Trainee pilots at Eastbourne during that period included Japanese (allies in that war), Brazilians and American servicemen. The aerodrome was classed as 'not at present on the list of permanent stations of the RAF', which links with some parliamentary questions mentioned later. There were 42 motor vehicles, including eight motorcycles with sidecars, and one touring car for the Commanding Officer. The works and buildings are described in much detail, from which it is obvious, firstly, that no women were accommodated within the airfield boundaries, and, secondly, that Fowler's original hangar was 69 ft square, the larger building was 179 ft × 59 ft, and that among other buildings were the Doping, Carpentry, Gunnery and Tyre Stores, Fabric Shops, Smith's Shop (for metal work), Lecture huts, and the Regimental Institute, in today's parlance, the Canteen.

At some time towards the end of the war, Fowler published a booklet of 21 photographs which included a staff group, dated July 1918, and pictures of four of the aircraft built at EAC (a BE2c, a Maurice Farman and two views of an Avro 504K) and of the office and workshops at the Seaplane Base. The distribution of the booklet must have been restricted to a relatively small number of copies, as only three have come to light since we began our researches. Some of the photographs, which provide a unique record of aircraft manufacture at this period, are illustrated on pages 91–99.

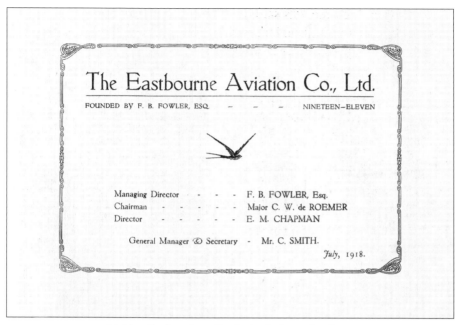

74. Frontispiece from Fowler's photograph album.

75. Staff group, July 1918.
Back row: unknown, Will Dowsett, unknown, unknown, unknown, unknown, unknown.
Seated: E. W. Willard, unknown, Charles Smith, unknown, Dick Dyer. *On ground:* unknown.

76. The General Office.

77. The Gas Engine and Generator (later used to power the Eastbourne tramway in the 1960s).

78. The Finished Parts Stores.

79. The Metal Machine Shop.

80. The Metal Fitting Shop.

81. The Wood Machine Shop.

82. The Wing Assembly Shop.

83. The Wing Covering Shop.

84. The Doping Shop.

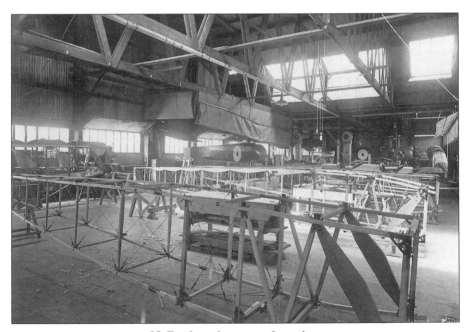

85. Fuselages in course of erection.

86. The Engine Fitting Shop.

87. The Erecting Shop.

88. An EAC-built BE2c biplane (1183), July 1915.

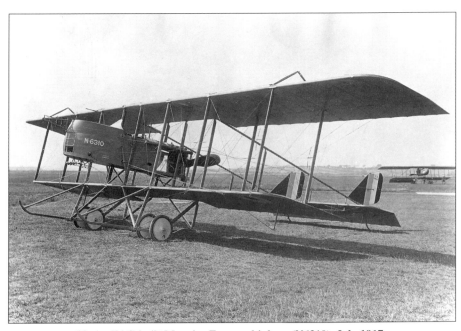

89. An EAC-built Maurice Farman biplane (N6310), July 1917.

90. An EAC-built Avro 504K (E4363), *c.* 1918.

During the 1939–45 war, the large hangar was used for storage by the Canadian Army, and in 1945 by Caffyns Ltd as a repair workshop for RAF vehicles. A photograph shows that it was later used as a furniture depository by Wenham's of Eastbourne Ltd. Latterly it was used by the Eastbourne Omnibus Society as a store for veteran buses until it was dismantled in late 1990.

Sidney Wenham also bought the RNAS Guard House, converting it into a bungalow for his own occupation. It still remains in use and is the last physical remnant of the EAC Aerodrome which remains *in situ.*

91. The large RNAS hangar, later used by Wenham's for storage.

92. The Guard House, Leeds Avenue, in 1998.

93. An EAC-built Avro 504K (H5240), later G-NZAB, at the Seaplane Base, 1919.

The final batch of Avro 504Ks (H5240–H5289) was ordered late in 1918. It is not certain if all were completed, but H5240 and H5241 were delivered to New Zealand in 1920 as part of the Imperial Gift. Part of the batch may have been delivered in the form of spares. The survey also mentions that Polegate Airfield was three miles to the north-west. This was the ex-RNAS (by then the RAF) airship station.

Eight EAC-built Avro 504Ks from the E4324–E4373 batch came on to the Civil Register in 1919 and were used as part of the Avro Transport Company's joy-riding fleet.

Fatalities associated with the Eastbourne RNAS/RAF Station

No less than 18 Eastbourne-based airmen lost their lives at the airfield, as well as three others who were in transit to or from other aerodromes. Of these, two were Australian, and one came from each of Brazil, Canada and the USA. One civilian working at the airfield was killed in an accident with an aircraft, as was an American engine fitter. A coroner's inquest was invariably held, details of which were reported in the local Press. We have recorded below, in chronological order, salient details from these reports[18].

10 March 1915: Probationary Flight Sub-Lieutenant Arthur Gelston Shepherd, RNAS, aged 21, of Boars Hill, Oxford, had taken his Pilot's Certificate some eight months previously, having flown at Hendon, Eastchurch and Sheppey. He took off in a biplane from the seaplane sheds with the intention of flying to the aerodrome at St Anthony's. He experienced difficulties soon afterwards and crashed into the sea some 300 yards offshore, turning upside down in the process. The inquest was unable to determine whether the accident was due to engine trouble or to a misjudgement of his height above the sea. Shepherd was buried at Wootton St Peter Church, Berks.

Eastbourne Gazette, 17 March 1915.

30 June 1915: Flight Sub-Lieutenant Preston Albert Watson, of Dundee, aged 34, was an RNAS trainee pilot, based at Eastchurch. Flying a Caudron GIII (3266) from Eastchurch to Eastbourne, he crashed heavily from a height of 200 ft in a field near to the Cross-in-Hand Hotel, north of Eastbourne, due either to the engine exploding or to a wing collapsing. The jury decided that the cause of death was not ascertainable. His body was taken to Dundee for burial.

Eastbourne Chronicle, 3 July 1915.

18 September 1915: On the evening of 14 September, an aeroplane piloted by Flight Lieutenant Hilton Jones with Flight Sub-Lieutenant William Croucher, RNAS, aged 19, as passenger, took off from the aerodrome and flew to Shoreham, where it remained overnight. Croucher, of Dulwich, a former civil servant at the Admiralty, had obtained his Pilot's Certificate some ten weeks previously. The next day they took off and arrived at about 5.30 pm at Bignor Park for a rendezvous with an army unit. While approaching the intended landing area, the pilot realised that it was unsuitable and tried to abort the landing. In doing so he probably misjudged the climb and speed of his machine and the engine may not have pulled up quickly enough to clear the surrounding trees. The pilot was reported to have said that the engine had stopped at the time of impact. Flight Lieutenant Hilton Jones was severely injured and hospitalised and his passenger, Flight Sub-Lieutenant Croucher, died three days later as a result of extensive brain injuries. He was interred at Chichester Cemetery, with six mechanics from Eastbourne Aerodrome acting as bearers.

Sussex Daily News, 22 September 1915.

10 January 1916: A Short S38 biplane (3148) flown by Probationary Flight Sub-Lieutenant Gordon Ezra Duke, a 20-year-old Canadian from Toronto, with his instructor, Warrant Officer (Second Grade) Percival Victor Fraser, a 30-year-old Australian from Queensland, took off from the aerodrome and soon started to fly irregularly. Their machine nose-dived from approximately 150 ft to crash near a brickfield at Hampden Park owned by Alderman Mark Martin, the local builder, killing both men. The cause of the accident was thought to be a wire which slipped off an elevator control pulley. The funeral of the two men took place at Ocklynge Cemetery three days later.

Eastbourne Gazette, 12 and 19 January 1916.

17 March 1917: Second Lieutenant David Dennys Fowler of 78 Squadron, RFC, aged 20, who had been educated at Harrow and Trinity College, Cambridge, died when his BE2c (7181) crashed near to the aerodrome. It was concluded that Fowler, who was an experienced pilot, had tried to turn in the air while the machine was too flat; in consequence the machine had nose-dived and struck the ground. A witness had found the aeroplane upside down on the ground in flames, with the deceased underneath. He was dead when rescuers were able to extricate him from the machine. Fowler's body was taken to St Margaret's Church, Rottingdean, for burial.

Eastbourne Chronicle, 24 March 1917.

16 June 1917: An Avro 504A (A9774), piloted by Lieutenant Henry Irving Newton, RFC, with Lieutenant Rupert Holton Herd, Australian Flying Corps, aged 25, an Australian from Ringwood, Victoria, as passenger *en route* from Upavon, overshot the runway at Eastbourne. The pilot restarted the engine intending to fly round the airfield and make a second attempt to land. However, the engine did not pick up very well and the aircraft lost speed and nose-dived into the ground. Upon impact, the petrol tank burst and the petrol caught fire with flames 100 ft high. Lieutenant Newton was able to scramble clear but Lieutenant Herd was pinned beneath the wreckage and it was thought that he was killed by the impact. Later his body was taken from the Town Hall mortuary to Ocklynge Cemetery by an escort of six cavalrymen from the Command Depot off Victoria Drive.

Eastbourne Gazette, 20 and 27 June 1917.

23 October 1917: Probationary Flight Lieutenant James Peter Crawford-Wood, with Probationary Observer Officer Kenneth Oxley, flying an Avro 504G (N5310) [some reports say a BE2c (9465)], from Eastchurch Flying School, died as a result of a crash near Eastbourne. Crawford-Wood's body was removed to Alkerton, Oxon, for burial.

Eastbourne Gazette, 31 October 1917.

28 January 1918: Ray O. Garver[19], a 26-year-old American cadet from 3 Training Squadron, flew a Sopwith Camel (B9282) from Shoreham to Eastbourne on Monday morning. An hour after landing, he began his return journey. A short distance after take-off his machine suddenly nose-dived into the ground near the Gas Works from a height of about 150 ft. The pilot was taken to the Military Hospital but died shortly after admission.

Eastbourne Gazette, 30 January 1918.

21 March 1918: Probationary Flight Officer Lewis Brown, aged 18, of Thornton-le-Fylde, was strapped into his aircraft on the runway waiting for his engine to be started when a Sopwith Camel (D6496), descending from about 1000 ft, landed on his machine. It appeared that Flight Officer Brown was struck on the head by the propeller or undercarriage of the landing machine, whose pilot's vision had been obstructed by the circle of the propeller of his machine. A verdict of accidental death was returned by the inquest jury, with no blame being attached to anyone. A few days later, Flight Officer Brown's body was returned to his home town of Blackpool for burial.

Eastbourne Gazette, 27 March 1918.

12 June 1918: Mr Frederick Walter Elstone, aged 38, a married man with four children, employed as a stockman-carter, of Hamland Farm, Huggetts Lane, Willingdon, was operating a mowing machine drawn by two horses at the aerodrome. He was killed when struck on the head by the propeller of an ascending aircraft flown by a Brazilian naval trainee pilot, Second Lieutenant Olavo de Araujo[20]. The inquest jury returned a verdict of accidental death but found that the pilot had not taken sufficient care to ensure that his path was clear for take-off. Mr Elstone's funeral took place at Willingdon Parish Church a few days later.

Some months later, in March 1919, Mrs Elstone, widow of the deceased, was awarded the sum of £280 under the Workmen's Compensation Act, taking into account the deceased's average weekly wage of something over £1/16s. (£1·80) per week.

Eastbourne Gazette, 19 June 1918 and *Eastbourne Chronicle,* 22 March 1919.

12 June 1918: Second Lieutenant William Stanley Pullen, 206 TDS, RAF (Eastbourne), aged 18, whose parents lived at Aston Manor, Birmingham, was killed whilst practising his third landing of the evening. His aircraft, an Avro 504A (D1606), had been built at EAC. When turning to come down, he involuntarily stalled his engine causing the aircraft to dive into the ground near to the Aylesbury Dairy, Langney, from a height of about 250 ft. The pilot was unconscious when Charles Colbran, employed at the dairy, reached the crash site and he died some forty minutes later. The accident was found to be due to the pilot's error of judgement and a verdict of death from misadventure was recorded. Pullen's body was taken to Upton-cum-Chalvey (Slough) for burial.

Eastbourne Gazette, 19 June 1918.

17 July 1918: Lieutenant Edward Moulton Parsons, RAF, of Bristol, who had been at the aerodrome for only two days, but who had previous flying experience, took a Camel (F1411) up for a practice flight on Wednesday evening. The aircraft was seen to be coming down from about 3000 ft in a spinning nose-dive but the pilot appeared to lose control for the last 400 ft and crashed. He was assumed to be dead by the time that help arrived. The inquest jury returned a verdict of accidental death due to an unknown cause. Parsons was buried at Bristol (Canford) Cemetery.

The deceased's elder brother had been awarded a posthumous VC in November 1917.

Eastbourne Gazette, 24 July 1918.

21 August 1918: Lieutenant Charles Albert Manzetti, RAF, a married man aged 25, of Clapham Park, London, took off from the airfield in a Sopwith Camel (B6446), painted a bright red, and circled two or three times before flying off towards the country. Minutes later the machine was seen by another pilot to be spinning down in the distance when it disappeared behind some trees. It crashed in a field near Fords Lane, Hankham, and Lieutenant Manzetti's body was later found in the wreckage. A military court of enquiry had satisfied itself that everything connected with the machine was in order and there was no accounting for the accident. The inquest jury brought in a verdict of accidental death. Lieutenant Manzetti was buried in Ocklynge Cemetery.

Eastbourne Gazette, 28 August 1918.

22 August 1918: Flight Cadet Robert Kirkwood Galloway, RAF, aged 23, took off from the airfield in an EAC-built Avro 504K (D1624) and was seen to circle it at no great speed or height. In trying to turn, the pilot evidently misjudged his speed and began to spin into the ground. After the accident the controls were examined and found to be in good order. The jury returned a verdict of accidental death.

Eastbourne Gazette, 28 August 1918.

29 August 1918: The first inquest to be held in Eastbourne without a jury heard the circumstances surrounding the death of Flight Cadet Philip George Dalton Winchester, 63 Training Squadron, RAF, a married man aged 24, of 4 Winchelsea Road, Eastbourne. Winchester had previously served with the 2nd King Edward's Horse in France. Lieutenant John Macrae, RAF, was in charge of a flight and had instructed Winchester to take out a Sopwith Camel (C8291) with which he was thoroughly familiar. He had seen him ascend and circle round and then fly away. He was later told that the fabric had come away from one of the wings in the air and the wing had then collapsed. Air Mechanic Frank Parker stated that at about 11.00 on Thursday morning he had seen the aeroplane at an altitude of about 1,000 ft. He noticed it dive, followed by an explosion, when both wings came away. Upon examination, it appeared that a patch on one of the wings had come off causing the fabric to strip away and the wing to collapse. The accident was to be considered by a special RAF committee. Several days later, after a service at Christ Church, the burial took place at Ocklynge Cemetery.

Eastbourne Gazette, 4 and 11 September 1918.

5 September 1918: A formation of six aeroplanes, three flown by Brazilian officers, took off from the airfield. The leader of the formation, Captain Frank H. Creasy, RAF, stated that they reached a height of about 1,500 ft when he saw Lieutenant Reginald Horace Sanders, aged 24, of 50 TDS (Eastbourne), piloting a Sopwith Camel (F3207) about 100 ft above First Lieutenant Eugenio da Silva Possolo, also aged 24, of the Brazilian navy, also in a Camel. Lieutenant Sanders started to descend to take his place in the formation about thirty yards to the side of Lieutenant Possolo. However he appeared to lose sight of the other aircraft and struck it to the rear and on top of it. Both machines crashed to the ground in a field near to a farmhouse at Friday Street, causing terrible injuries to both men. Two of the other aircraft, a Sopwith Pup painted with black and white stripes and an Avro, landed on the adjacent common. The pilots got out and ran over to the wreckage, to find the two men dead. The Coroner expressed the view that no blame was attached to either officer and the jury returned a verdict of accidental death. After a burial service, Lieutenant Possolo was interred at Ocklynge Cemetery. Prior to the interment of Lieutenant Sanders at Hampstead Cemetery, a service was held at St Stephen's Church, Haverstock Hill, London NW.

Lieutenant Sanders had served since 1914 with the Royal Engineers in the Dardanelles and in Egypt, taking part in the capture of Jerusalem. He had transferred to the RFC in October 1917 and was still completing his training. His parents, Dr and Mrs Sanders, were living at Valetta, King's Drive, Hampden Park, Eastbourne.

Eastbourne Gazette, 11 September 1918.

5 September 1918: Second Lieutenant William Rhodes Barnett, RAF, aged 27, of Shrewsbury, had served formerly with the King's Shropshire Light Infantry. He took off for an afternoon flight and his Sopwith Camel was seen to be going well, having been used by other aviators earlier in the day. A witness, Charles Levitt, on the ground at nearby Hailsham, saw the aircraft come out of the clouds at a great height and loop-the-loop. When doing a second loop, the aircraft seemed 'to get on his back' and was unable to recover. The machine then started to descend very rapidly and crashed into a wood. When Mr Levitt reached the aircraft, he found Lieutenant Barnett dead, still strapped in his seat. The deceased had been instructed prior to take-off not to loop-the-loop. The verdict of the jury was accidental death, no defects having been found on the aeroplane. Barnett was buried at Wenlock (Broseley) Cemetery in Shropshire.

Eastbourne Gazette, 11 September 1918.

During the course of the last two inquests, the Coroner, Mr G. Vere Benson, commented upon the fact that fatalities have been numerous of late, and he added that the evidence in most cases suggested that the pilots were a little more adventurous than was perhaps necessary. There had been no evidence that anything was wrong with the machines in which they were flying. At one enquiry he had held, it was explained that a machine fell in flames upon a house which was nearly set on fire. He thought that the authorities might impress upon young and ardent airmen that it would be better for them to be adventurous where there was the least chance of their doing harm to other people.

Eastbourne Gazette, 11 September 1918.

13 October 1918: Lieutenant Charles Robert Chapman, RAF, aged 19, was flying on Sunday morning, and after performing some evolutions his aircraft was seen to dive and strike the ground. The cause of death was given as a fracture of the base of the skull. Sitting without a jury, the Coroner returned a verdict of death by misadventure. Lieutenant Chapman was buried at Ocklynge Cemetery.

Eastbourne Gazette, 16 October 1918.

10 November 1918: Private Hugh Hancock Hamill, aged 19, from Pueblo, Colorado, was serving with the American Air Service at the Eastbourne Airfield as an engine fitter. His duties were to assist in taking aircraft out onto the runways and swinging the propellers to start them. On 7 November Private Hamill was swinging the propeller of an aircraft which was waiting to ascend when it threw him up and struck him on the legs. On admittance to the Military Hospital, examination revealed serious injuries to both legs. By 9 November gas gangrene had developed in both wounds and despite amputation of his left leg, the organism had got into his blood stream and Private Hamill died the next day. Ground staff and the pilot confirmed that the engine switch had been in the off position at the time of the accident and nothing faulty had been found in the wiring system. The jury found that the accident was unavoidable and that death was due to gas gangrene in the leg wounds. Ironically, Private Hamill died the day before the armistice was signed.

Eastbourne Gazette, 20 November 1918.

As can be seen, there were many hazards associated with aviation during these war years, even under training conditions. It has often been said that the life expectancy of a pilot on the Western Front under battle conditions was measurable in days rather than weeks. We must admire and respect these young men for their courage and strength of purpose during this period of history which set the foundations for the safe era of aviation which we now enjoy.

1. Iron, D.: I learnt to fly on a Boxkite, *Aeroplane Monthly,* January 1975.

2. Kempston was a large private house situated at No 3 Grassington Road and was used as a temporary hospital during the war. It still stands and is now divided into flats.

3. Ashworth, C. (1990): *Action Stations 9: Military Airfields of the Central South and South East.*

4. Sturtivant, R. and Page, G. (1992): *Royal Naval Aircraft Serials and Units 1911–1919.*

5. Layman, R. D. (1989): *Before the Aircraft Carrier: the Development of Aviation Vessels 1849–1922.*

6. Roskill, S. W. (1969): *The Navy Air Service, Vol 1, 1908–1918.*

7. Jones, H. A. and Raleigh, Sir W. (1928): *The War in the Air* (6 vols).

8. Burns, I. and Nailer, R.: HMS *Vindex, Cross and Cockade International,* Vol 17, No 3 (1986).

9. Both sources are in error in giving Fowler the rank of Flight Commander. He was still a Flight Lieutenant at this date.

10. A piece of aircraft fabric with the Caffyn symbol and the words 'Engineers, Aircraft Manufacturers, Eastbourne' was recovered from an SE5a which crashed in Polygon Wood, Ypres, in 1918 and is now

displayed in the boardroom at Eastbourne. Caffyns were subcontractors to one of the larger firms, such as Wolseley or Austin, who constructed the aircraft and, as such, completed 75 sets of wings, ailerons and rudders only.

11. The fumes from the dopes were extremely toxic and *Flight* would from time to time report on fatalities resulting from their inhalation.

12. Early in 1999, planning permission was granted for a block of flats to be erected on the Eversley Court site. This will necessitate demolition of the building.

13. Sandwell, A. H. (via Molson K. M.): War-time Reminiscences, *Cross and Cockade Great Britain,* Vol 13, No 1 (1982).

14. Cole, C. and Cheesman E. F. (1984): *The Air Defence of Britain 1914–1918.*

15. Crundall, E. D. (1975): *Fighter Pilot on the Western Front.*

16. Travers, E. (1995): *Cross Country.*

17. The two types of aircraft are interesting, showing standardisation. Earlier, in October 1915, the station had various types: seven Blériots, three Caudron G.III, seven Curtiss JN3, four Grahame-White XV, two Henry Farman, four Maurice Farman, two White and Thompson 'Bognor Bloaters', a Bristol TB8, and a BE2c (see Appendix 16). In August and September 1916, the one and only prototype Wight Landplane (N501) was used briefly until it was written off in a crash in September 1916.

    Goodall, M. H.: Eastbourne Aviation Company 1911–1924: *Air Pictorial,* March 1979.

    Lewis, P. (1980): *The British Bomber since 1914.*

18. Details of airmen's deaths have been amplified by reference to: Hobson, C. (1995): *Airmen died in the Great War 1914-1918,* the records of the Commonwealth War Graves Commission and the memoirs left by Mr Tapp. In cases where differences have been found, these records have been preferred to those of the local Press.

19. Springs, E. W. (1927): *War Birds – Diary of an Unknown Aviator* refers to him as Roy Garver.

20. Araujo later attained the rank of Admiral in the Brazilian navy. See Hart, K.: Brazilians in Britain – 1918, *Cross and Cockade Great Britain,* Vol 16, No 2 (1985).

After the War

The EAC directorships by July 1918 are of interest, bearing in mind that the von Roemer family changed its name from the German style to the more acceptable style of de Roemer during the war, and we now find the following:

Major Charles William de Roemer (Electrical Engineer of Herstmonceux), Chairman.

Major F. B. Fowler, Managing Director.

Rowland E. B. Hunt.

Edward Mayo Chapman, 9 Milnthorpe Road, Eastbourne.

Charles Henry de Roemer, formerly Baron C. H. von Roemer.

Charles Smith, General Manager and Secretary.

Hugh Winfield Roll, solicitor, of Midland Bank Chambers and 4 Southdown House, Eastbourne.

Blanche Hucks, wife of Frank Hucks, now of 201 Brecknock Road, Tufnell Park, London N19.

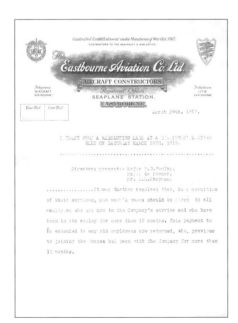

94. The Directors' Resolution, March 1919.

At a Directors' Meeting held on Saturday 29 March 1919, the following resolution was passed: 'that, in recognition of their services, one week's wages should be given to all employees . . . who have been in its employ for more than 12 months'.

By 1919, Major Fowler assumed the secretaryship of the EAC, replacing Charles Smith, who remained as General Manager at the Seaplane Base factory. Society of British Aircraft Constructors membership continued, being down-graded to Associate rank in 1921 and ceasing altogether in 1923.

In the King's Birthday Honours List of Friday 13 June 1919, Major Fowler was awarded the Air Force Cross, a decoration, instituted in June 1918, which recognised 'acts of valour, courage or devotion to duty whilst flying, though not in active operations against the enemy'. Fowler also took out a 'B' Class Private Pilot's Licence (No 86) in November 1920, which entitled him to fly Avro 504s and Short 184s.

Many years later, another memory of Eastbourne Airfield came from Squadron Leader H. E. Hervey, MC, who had flown as an observer with the legendary WW1 air ace, Captain Albert Ball, VC, DSO, MC. He had the distinction of being the Commanding Officer of Britain's first glider unit, No 1 Glider Training School, at Thame, Oxfordshire, where Gerald Newson served under his command when the unit opened in 1941. Hervey recalled that in 1919 he flew to Eastbourne to have lunch with a wartime colleague. Upon returning from lunch they found some American airmen, who were in Eastbourne awaiting shipment home, trying to start his aeroplane so that they could enjoy what they called 'a flip'.

The airfield was still occasionally used by the RAF after the war as is evidenced by the following article from the local Press:

Aeroplane in a Ditch

Mishap at Eastbourne

After a forced landing, caused by engine trouble, a service machine that descended at the RAF Flying Ground, Eastbourne, came to grief in a well-watered ditch. The 'plane, a 'baby' Handley Page, carrying five officers and two other ranks, had come from Andover and touched Reading and Hastings on its way. It would have gone on to Winchester but for a mishap to its starboard engine, and it was decided to come down at Eastbourne. The machine safely reached

95. A Handley Page in a ditch at the EAC airfield, 1919.

the ground, but some difficulty was then experienced in bringing it to a standstill. It jumped a dyke and at one time looked like charging a large haystack close to the main road. This danger was happily averted, but in its expiring movements the 'plane finished with its undercarriage in a ditch. Fortunately none of the passengers was injured. The aeroplane, which was little damaged, was left where it was, pending the arrival of a 'crash crew'.

Eastbourne Chronicle, 20 September 1919.

A report of an interview with Major Fowler appeared in the *Sussex County Herald* on 26 July 1919. The reporter was shown round the factory and initiated into the technicalities of aircraft construction. He reported that the principal woods used were English ash and silver spruce, selected for their even grain; that safety considerations impacted upon every aspect of construction; and that every part of the aircraft except the engines were made at the works. He went on to quote Major Fowler's statement that 'passenger work is being carried out at Eastbourne, Bexhill, Worthing and Brighton and, as soon as existing restrictions are removed, it is hoped to run a cross-channel service between Eastbourne and Boulogne'. They also hoped to open up the flying school again, as soon as the Government gave up the aerodrome.

In January 1920 Fowler had tried to stir interest in a special 'School of Flying for Ladies', giving air-experience flights to some potential

96. Lieutenant Loton with lady pupils, 1920.

pupils. Fowler's charge for tuition leading to a private licence was £125, while a commercial licence cost £300. Earlier than that he had arranged to loop-the-loop with a reporter named Madelaine St Clair, whose double column account in *The Mercury* of Friday 22 August 1919 savours of the spirit of early flying.

97. EAC aerial photograph of the Redoubt. The airfield can be seen top right.

Other reports appeared in the *Sunday Pictorial* of 25 January 1920, the *Weekly Illustrated Sunday Herald* of 25 January, the *Eastbourne Gazette* of 28 January, the *Lady's Pictorial* of 6 March, and other sources, so one cannot but concede that Fowler spread his publicity net far and wide. The Company also advertised its aerial photography service, a product of which was published in *Flight* on 4 December 1919.

The Company also began to offer motor-car coachwork, painting and repairs 'under the management of Mr C. Smith, late of Caffyns Ltd' as advertisements in the *Eastbourne Gazette* in May 1919 and December 1922 demonstrate.

The Avro Joy-Riding Fleet

As aircraft construction for military contracts ended in 1919, the Board decided to restart joy rides, which were again becoming popular. Minutes of the Council's Watch Committee meeting on 4 March 1919 record that a number of companies had applied for permission to inaugurate local aircraft services and that Major Fowler, who had recently combined his Eastbourne Aviation Company with the Gosport Aircraft Company, should be invited to meet the committee to discuss the matter. Minutes of the next meeting on 13 March reported that the Gosport Aircraft Company was now incorporated with the EAC so far as aerial coastal trips were concerned. The Minutes went on to recommend that Major Fowler's company should be allocated three bays of the foreshore opposite the end of Cambridge Road and also, at times of high water, a bay between groynes slightly to the west of the Wish Tower. The Company would be required to pay a commission to the Council at the rate of 5% of the fees taken.

The joy-riding fleet began with two Sunbeam-built Avro 504Ks and two J. S. White-built Short 184s, the latter converted by EAC into 4-seater aircraft. Later there were no less than eight Avros, in addition to the two Shorts (see Appendix 17). The aircraft were painted a brilliant red. In order to advertise the activity, the Company, in August 1919, joined with the *Sussex County Herald* to run a weekly draw for which there were six prizes consisting of an aeroplane ride for the price of £1, weather permitting. The winners during the first four weeks included:

Mrs C. M. Woods of Willingdon Road
Miss Lesley Merrick of London
Dorothy Green of New Upperton Road
Miss Eunice Burbridge of Gildredge Road
Nellie Lewis of Cavendish Avenue
Alfred Moss of Hailsham
R. Jervis of Horeham Road
Joan Kirby of Clarence Road
Mrs M. Loftus of Cambridge Road
Miss Botting of Lewes
Miss G. M. Howell of Prideaux Road
Frank Shuter of Susans Road
W. Gardener of Hyde Road
T. G. Saunderson of Langney Road
Mrs G. Humble Crofts of Waldron
Mrs Cannon of Terminus Road
Mrs A. Jackson of Terminus Place

Miss M. Beal of Uckfield
E. R. Boniface of New Road
W. Adams of London
Mrs Vere Hudson of Lewes
Geo. J. Smith of Lewes
R. Underwood of Mayfield Place
Mrs S. A. Hide of Taddington Road

Several of the winners were sufficiently enthusiastic about their experiences in the air to record their impressions for the newspaper; one, the husband of a lucky winner, even composed a lengthy poem.

Fowler's long-time acquaintance, Wing Commander A. G. Loton, AFC, in a letter to Gerald Newson, recalled: 'Early in 1919 Fowler asked me to become a pilot instructor at Eastbourne, and I left the RAF to take up that appointment. The EAC also built two Avro 504L seaplanes, modified to take two passengers behind the pilot, which flew from Eastbourne beach near the Queen's Hotel. I took one of these to Brighton to give flights in 1919, returning to Eastbourne at the end of the season. I went back to Brighton again in 1920, but at the end of that season we could not carry on and I left EAC at that time, though I kept in touch with Fowler'.

EAC in fact built six Avro 504L seaplanes, retaining two for their own use, as stated by Wing Commander Loton. One (G-EAJH), which he was piloting, sank off Hove on 19 August 1920 with a collapsed undercarriage, following a seaplane race held as a finale to the Hove Regatta and Carnival. Another of the EAC 504Ls went to Sweden and was still flying in 1928.

COUPON.   AUG. 2nd
FOR
FREE TRIPS by SEAPLANE
or AEROPLANE
Arranged by the
Sussex County Herald

To the Secretary,
The Sussex County Herald,
EASTBOURNE.
I should like to participate in the drawing for Free Seaplane or Aeroplane Flights, arranged by the "SUSSEX COUNTY HERALD"
And I agree to abide by the conditions.

Signed ....

Address ....

....

....

I prefer to take my flight next ....

N.B. This coupon must reach the office of the "SUSSEX COUNTY HERALD" by Tuesday morning next.

Mark the top left hand corner of the envelope "Flight."

98. Advertisement for the Prize Draw, *Sussex County Herald*, 2 August 1919.

115

99. The Avro Joy-Riding Fleet, 1920.

The *Brighton Herald* of 21 August 1920 gives a vivid account of the Hove incident:

'There was a quite dramatic but unrehearsed effect given at the finish of the regatta. The three seaplanes had just finished a race when one machine, which was piloted by Mr A. G. Loton and also carried a mechanic named Nicholas, made the crowd hold their breath. The machine had almost completed a steep banking turn, when the nose dropped, hit the sea very heavily, and remained afloat with its tail pointing to the sky.

Two little figures could be seen scrambling out of the cockpits, and a yell went up from the crowd to a motor boatman, who went to the rescue with several other small craft that happened to be out. One of the seaplanes landed beside the wreck, but took off again and signalled to the shore that the men were safe as it bid farewell to the crowds and went off home to Eastbourne.

100. G-EAJH before the crash.

After some anxious waiting, the crowds suddenly rushed *en masse* to the edge of the water. They had seen a boat making for the shore, and wanted to see the airmen land. But they were not in the boat! It was only a party that had been out for a row. The airmen came in later, and eventually the wrecked machine was towed ashore and safely beached. It was fortunate that the sea was calm, or the machine would not have remained afloat. Had it sunk the loss would have been heavy, for this particular type of seaplane costs anything from £1,500 to £2,000 each.'

In fact no less than four of the Avros crashed, while the two Shorts were scrapped in August 1920.

Eastbourne Council Minutes of 16 April 1920 record that the amount paid in respect of commission on seaplane flights amounted to £84/18/11 [£84·95].

101. Lieutenant Loton's crash at Hove, 1920.

Given that the rate of commission was 5%, this suggests that the season's takings for flights off the Eastbourne beach were £1,699.

The Sempill Mission to Japan

Wing Commander Loton's letter continued: 'In 1921, Fowler told me that he was going to Japan with Colonel the Master of Sempill's mission which was to organise and train the Imperial Japanese Navy's Flying Branch. He was to be in charge of flying, and I went as Instructor in Elementary Flying Training. The advance party, including Fowler and myself [with Max ('Tommy') Ford as mechanic], left for Japan early in 1921, on a year's contract initially. [A copy of Max Ford's letter of appointment, signed by Colonel Sempill, is at Appendix 18. It is interesting to note his salary during the term of the contract, £400, quite a respectable income in those days.] Fowler came home at the end of the year, but I stayed on until February 1923, both Fowler and I being awarded the Imperial Order of the Rising Sun (4th Class)'.

The widow of one of the men recalled to Gerald Newson that the party also included Messrs Bond, Crisp, Earmaker, Ellis, Hunter,

102. The Sempill Mission to Japan: Colonel Sempill seated centre, Major Fowler on his right, Max Ford 5th from left, back row.

Kearton, J. Machin, W. Machin, Redwood, Satchell and J. Manton. In March 1922 the party sailed on the *Aquitania* to New York, whence they travelled overland to Seattle before boarding a Japanese vessel. The aircraft were crated and then sent to Japan by sea on the easterly route through the Suez Canal. The party operated from about 22 July 1922 at a base named Kasumigaura, some 50 miles from Tokyo. Their aircraft fleet included some Sparrowhawks, ten A.V. Roe Hamble-built Avro 504Ls (one a seaplane) and a Parnell Panther. The instructors included Major Orde-Lees and Mr H. Crisp. On 3 September 1921, they made a mass formation flight to escort the Crown Prince's warship and alighted in Yokosuka harbour. The late Jack Warne, whose father worked for the EAC as an instructor in the Dope Shop[1], recalled[2] Fowler and Ford coming to his house after their return from Japan and showing him an album of snapshots including one, taken from the air, of HMS *Renown* entering Yokohama harbour with the Prince of Wales, accompanied by his cousin, Lieutenant Lord Louis Mountbatten, on board. A similar album has been generously lent to us by Wallace James Ford, Max's nephew. It contains a collection of photographs of the party's travels in Japan and through Hong Kong, Singapore, Malacca, Colombo, the Suez Canal and the Mediterranean, as well as a number of rarely seen photographs of aircraft at Eastbourne. A number of these have, with Mr Ford's permission, been reproduced in this publication.

The De-commissioning of the Airfield

Notice to Airmen No 135, issued by the Air Ministry and dated 9 December 1920, states that the airfield (as distinct from the Seaplane Base) had been removed from the list of authorised airfields, as EAC had given up the lease, as recorded by Wing Commander Loton. In late 1921, construction was switched, using the Seaplane Base, from aircraft to a new type of small, lightweight car, plus a number of large charabancs to be mounted on an ex-Army chassis. Unfortunately, after a number of these had been constructed, they were found to contravene Ministry of Transport permitted width by six inches, so the contract was cancelled. The three main buildings on this site were a seaplane shed, 180 ft × 60 ft, another 180 ft × 40 ft, and a Joinery and Paint Shop of 140 ft × 40 ft, providing a large working area in total.

The Aeroplane of 30 March and 6 April 1921 carried brief and slightly facetious articles deploring the current state of the Eastbourne Aerodrome and stating that, since Major Fowler had relinquished the lease, someone had removed many of the boards covering the ditches. The author stated that 'quite a number of machines use this aerodrome as a port of call' and that it was someone's responsibility (he wasn't sure whose) to maintain the field in a safe condition. This may well have given rise to the exchanges described below, though as both Fowler and the RAF had relinquished responsibility for the airfield, it is difficult to see who else might have been responsible.

A Parliamentary Question

Eastbourne Airfield was soon the subject of a Parliamentary Question. On 7 April 1921, Mr Raper[3] asked the Secretary of State, 'Who is responsible for the Eastbourne Aerodrome, and why the same has not been retained by the Air Ministry as a supplementary landing ground, in view of the fact that this aerodrome, besides being one of the oldest in the United Kingdom, is in the most important geographical position from the point of view of commercial aviation; and whether the Air Ministry notice, dated 1 April 1921, cancelling the *Notice to Airmen No 135*, dated 9 December 1920, indicated that this aerodrome is again fit for use?'.

Mr McCurdy, Joint Parliamentary Secretary to the Treasury, stated, 'I have been asked to reply. This aerodrome was licensed to the Eastbourne Aviation Company, who asked for a cancellation of the licence in December last, and have since demolished the aerodrome. It was considered, with others, from the point of view of retention by the Air Ministry, but the circumstances did not justify its selection for that purpose. The answer to the last part of the question is in the negative'.

Mr Raper, 'Is it not a fact that notice was issued on 1 April cancelling No 135?'.

Mr McCurdy, 'I must ask for notice of that question'.

Not satisfied with this lack of information, Mr Raper asked on 12 April, of the Secretary of State for Air, 'For what purpose *Notice to Airmen No 135* was cancelled if Eastbourne Aerodrome is not now available for air traffic, in view of the fact that the cancellation of the notice referred to indicates that airmen can again land and take off safely at that ground?'.

Mr McCurdy, 'The Notice in question was cancelled because the periodical list of aerodromes to which it was a correction was also cancelled. The current periodical list does not include the Eastbourne Aerodrome'.

Undeterred, the questioner went on, 'Is it not a fact that the cancellation of that order has given rise to misapprehension?'.

Mr McCurdy, 'There appears to be no ground for that misapprehension'.

These exchanges certainly did not bring Eastbourne Aviation Company nor its airfield to life again.

Funds for the EAC had been obtained on 5 March 1920 by debenture from Barclays Bank Limited. The only directors by 31 December 1921 were Fowler, C. W. de Roemer and H. W. Roll, solicitor. Charles William de Roemer had been a Director since the formation of the Company. An Etonian, he had served in the RFC during the war, reaching the rank of Major, and was a notably inventive engineer; one of his early achievements was to build his own electrical plant at Lime Park, Herstmonceux, from which he supplied electricity to Herstmonceux village. The de Roemers, father and son, were directly descended from Baron Carl von Roemer of the House of Untersteinpleis in Saxony. Charles de Roemer's father, Baron von Roemer, born in London in 1866, had been an Honorary Major in the 3rd Sussex Militia and had married in 1886 a Mary Combe, of Oaklands, Sedlescombe, in Sussex.

Failure

In 1920 one of the airfield buildings (Shed No 3) was sold to the parish of Mayfield in East Sussex, a timber building to be used as the daughter-church at Five Ashes, now known as the Church of the Good Shepherd. They paid £250 for the structure, which was dedicated by the Bishop of Chichester on 8 November 1921, and is still in exemplary repair and active use to this day, though much of the original cladding has been replaced. The Five Ashes Parish minute book for 1920[4] gives a good account of the fundraising, acquisition, removal, re-erection and consecration of this relic of Eastbourne aviation history. Another shed

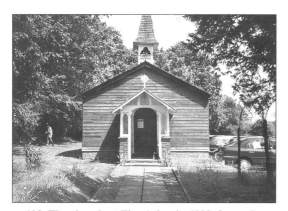

103. The church at Five Ashes in 1999, formerly No 3 Shed, EAC.

was sold to a Mr Bourne of Deanlands Road, Golden Cross (12 miles north of Eastbourne), where it was used for breeding rabbits[5]. Another wooden building which had stood opposite the guard house in Leeds Avenue was removed to Sidney Wenham's farm at Dittons Road, Polegate, where it was used as a bungalow until 1972[6].

By 16 December 1922, the Company's address was Royal Parade East, Eastbourne, and it was obvious that failure was in sight. On that date the bank appointed George Whitefield Plummer, Chartered Accountant, of 69 Terminus Road, Eastbourne, as the Receiver of the Company.

By July 1924, all work had ceased, and a well-known local firm, Edgar Horn, auctioned the machines and tools of the Company, realising £1,552. Neither aircraft nor buildings were included in the sale.

On 29 December 1925 the Entertainments and Pleasure Grounds Committee of Eastbourne Corporation discussed the purchase of the buildings. On 13 January 1926 the Receiver informed the Town Clerk that the buildings covered in total 33,000 square ft. A purchase price of £1,109/12s/11d (£1,109·65) was agreed on 4 February, with Mr Warren, solicitor, of Hillman Burt & Warren acting for the Receiver. The buildings were insured until 25 December 1927 with The Scottish Insurance Corporation Ltd, in the sum of £5,350, at an annual premium of £13/7s/6d (£13·38).

Municipal Eastbourne records that £300 was spent on alterations to make the sheds suitable for the storage and repair of deckchairs and the laundering of bathing towels.

Mr G. W. Plummer ceased to be the Receiver on 26 June 1926, and the Company finally ceased to exist, in the eyes of the law, on 8 November 1932.

An interesting footnote to this history of the Eastbourne Airfield is a report in the local Press[7] to the effect that Sir Alan Cobham landed in a 12-seater De Havilland DH61, the 'Youth of Britain', at the north end of the old aerodrome at Langney in 1929 as a part of his Municipal Aerodrome campaign. In fact, Cobham also brought his National Aviation Day display to Eastbourne in August 1932, August 1933 and in July 1935, though he used the King's Drive and Wilmington landing grounds on these occasions.

Fowler's Later Years

Major Fowler, not surprisingly, did not enter into aviation management again, and lived most of his remaining life in a pleasant part of Hampshire at Hinton St Michael near Christchurch. In 1934 Major and Mrs Fowler leased a large property known as East Close, which was a part of the Hinton Admiral Manor and turned it into an hotel which they ran until 1955. They then retired to live at the nearby East Close Cottage until their deaths. During this period, Fowler enjoyed sailing in the waters off Calshot where he had crashed so many years before.

104. East Close Hotel, near Christchurch, in 1999.

105. East Close Cottage in 1999.

He died in St Saviour's Hospital, Hythe, Kent, on 20 June 1967, aged 84, and was cremated at Barham Crematorium, Kent, on 23 June, his ashes being interred in the grave of an associated family at Saltwood Church, near Hythe. His will, proved on 20 September 1967, left the sum of £2,915/9s/0d (£2,915·45) which, after a small bequest to his wife's nephew, went to his wife Pleasance.

A dispassionate analysis of the rise and fall of the EAC identifies a number of factors which were significant. On the positive side, Bernard

Fowler was a skilled and meticulous engineer, an enterprising businessman and a brave and capable airman. It is possible that EAC was under-capitalised and maybe inadequately managed financially. When compared to more prosperous ventures at, say, Brooklands and Hendon, it was later on the scene and geographically more remote. Although in the days up to the outbreak of war Fowler worked assiduously to publicise it (there must, for example, have been regular Press reports sent to *Flight*), it never appeared as more than a minor player in this great new industry. None of Fowler's EAC designed planes proved saleable; if just one had emerged as a commercial success, the story might have been very different.

The coming of the war in 1914 closed the civil development of the airfield and took Fowler away from EAC. Aeroplane construction at the Seaplane Base switched to military contracts, but it must be questioned, given the Company's financial decline, whether this work was adequately profitable.

Once the war was over there seemed to be an almost frantic quest for revenue-generating activities: flying tuition, joy-riding, motor-car maintenance, car and charabanc construction, aerial photography – none of which, in a hostile economic climate, was successful in keeping the EAC afloat. Four Avros crashed and these may well have been uninsured. In addition, the two Short seaplanes were scrapped (see Appendix 17).

In 1921 Fowler went to Japan for a year and it has to be assumed that he had by then seen the writing on the wall, for the Company went into receivership a year later.

Thus does the story of Major Fowler and the EAC come to the end of a journey which embraced almost every aspect of pioneering aviation – civil, RNAS, RFC, RAF, home and abroad, manufacturing and flying, teaching and training, land and sea.

There are more illustrious pioneers of early aviation than Fowler, but none more inspired by ambition and courage. But for the run of the financial mill, he might have become one of the great names of aviation history.

That is sufficient reason for recording his story in this book, in the hope that the Eastbourne Aviation Company and Frederick Bernard Fowler, AFC, may not be forgotten.

1. In a letter to Michael Goodall in 1982, Jack Warne recalled memories of his father, who worked for the EAC from 1914 to 1919: 'My father was a fabric fitter, being an upholsterer and cabinet maker by trade. Then he was put in charge of the dope shop, instructing and supervising the girl staff who did this job. My father was an extremely able and conscientious man and he and all the family seemed to live for the Eastbourne Aviation Company in those days. My father lived to the age of 101, dying in 1979'.

2. *Eastbourne Local History Society Newsletter*, No 47, March 1983.

3. Alfred Baldwin Raper, born in 1889, served as a pilot during World War I and may thus have known Major Fowler. Raper was decorated by the Russians for services to the Russian Air Mission, and was Conservative Unionist MP for East Islington (London) from 1918 to 1922. He lived at Gerrards Cross, Buckinghamshire, and died in 1941.

4. Courtesy Mr T. Biron of Five Ashes.

5. This information based on Mr G. Clark's comments to the authors.

6. Information per letters from Sidney and Betty Wenham to Michael Goodall, 1973.

7. *Eastbourne Chronicle*, 6 July, 17 and 24 August 1929.

References

Newspapers and Periodicals

Aeroplane, The

Aeroplane Monthly

Air Pictorial

Brighton Herald, The

Christchurch Times, The

Cross and Cockade Great Britain Journal

Cross and Cockade International Journal

Eastbourne Chronicle

Eastbourne Civic Society Newsletter

Eastbourne Gazette

Eastbourne Herald

Eastbourne Local History Society Newsletter

Eastbournian, The

Flight

Gowland's Directories

Hansard

Kelly's Directories

Lady's Pictorial

London Gazette

Mayfield Parish Magazine

Mercury, The

Old Eastbournian, The

RAF Flying Review, The

Sunday Pictorial

Sussex County Herald

Sussex Daily News

Times, The

Weekly Despatch

Weekly Illustrated Sunday Herald

Books

Armstrong, R. (1979) *Wings over Eastbourne,* pub. privately.

Ashworth, C. (1990) *Actions Stations 9: Military Airfields of the Central South and South East,* Patrick Stephens.

Baring, M. (1968) *Flying Corps Headquarters 1914–1918,* Blackwood.

Barker, R. (1966) *Great Mysteries of the Air,* Chatto & Windus.

Barnes, C. H. (1976) *Handley Page Aircraft since 1907,* Putnam.

Bowyer, C. (1998) *Royal Flying Corps Communiqués 1917–1918,* Grub Street.

Brett, R. Dallas (1934) The *History of British Aviation 1908–1914,* (2 vols) John Hamilton.

Brooks, R. (1992) *Sussex Flights and Flyers 1919–1983, Downside Publications.*

Brown, A. (1998) *They flew from the New Forest,* pub. privately.

Bruce, J. M. (1957) *British Aeroplanes 1914–1918,* Putnam.

Bruce, J. M. (1982) *Aeroplanes of the RFC (Military Wing.),* Putnam.

Burke's Peerage (1904) *History of the Landed Gentry of Ireland,* Harrison & Sons.

Cole, C. (ed) (1990) *Royal Flying Corps Communiqués 1915–1916,* Tom Donovan.

Cole, C. (ed) (1990) *Royal Air Force Communiqués 1918,* Tom Donovan.

Cole, C. and Cheesman, E. F. (1984) *The Air Defence of Britain 1914–1918,* Putnam.

Crundall, E. D. (1975) *Fighter Pilot on the Western Front,* Wm. Kimber.

Fovargue, H. W. (1933) *Municipal Eastbourne,* Eastbourne Borough Council.

Fowler, S., Elliott, P., Nesbit, R. C. and Goulter, C. (1994) *RAF Records in the PRO,* PRO Publications.

Gowans, L. M. (1983) *The Story of Caffyns from 1865,* Caffyns plc.

Henshaw, T. (1995) *The Sky their Battlefield,* Grub Street.

Higham, R. (1960) *Britain's Imperial Air Routes 1918–1939,* Foulis.

Hobson, C. (1995) *Airmen died in the Great War 1914–1918,* J. B. Hayward.

Hurst, S. C. (1929) *The Silent Cities: an illustrated Guide to the War Cemeteries and Memorials in France and Flanders, 1914–1918,* Methuen.

Jackson, A. J. (1968) *Blackburn Aircraft since 1909,* Putnam.

Jackson, A. J. (1973) *British Civil Aircraft since 1919, vols 1–3,* Putnam.

Jackson, A. J. (1990) *Avro Aircraft since 1908,* Putnam.

Jackson, A. S. (1995) *Imperial Airways and the First British Airlines 1919–1940,* Terence Dalton.

Jones, H. A. (1923) *Over the Balkans and South Russia: being the History of 47 Squadron, Royal Air Force,* Edward Arnold.

Jones, H. A. and Raleigh, Sir W. (1928) *The War in the Air (6 vols),* Oxford UP.

Jones, I. (1954) *Tiger Squadron,* W. H. Allen.

Killen, J. (1969) *A History of Marine Aviation,* Fred. Muller.

Layman, R. D. (1989) *Before the Aircraft Carrier: the Development of Aviation Vessels 1849–1922,* Conway Maritime Press.

Learmonth, B., Nash, J. and Cluett, D. (1977) *The First Croydon Airport 1915–1928,* Sutton Libraries and Arts Services.

Lewis C. (1994) *Sagittarius Rising,* Warner Books.

Lewis G. (1976) *Wings over the Somme,* Wm. Kimber.

Lewis P. (1962) *British Aircraft 1809–1914,* Putnam.

Lewis P. (1979) *The British Fighter since 1912,* Putnam.

Lewis P. (1980) *The British Bomber since 1914,* Putnam.

McInnes, I. and Webb, J. V. (1991) *A Contemptible Little Flying Corps,* The London Stamp Exchange.

Middleton, E. (1920) *The Great War in the Air (4 vols),* Waverley Book Co.

Ogilvy, D. (1982) *The Shuttleworth Collection,* Airlife Publishing.

Owen, C. (1919) *Salonica and After,* Hodder & Stoughton.

Owen, G. (1959) *Around East Close,* pub. privately.

Penrose, H. (1972) *British Aviation – The Pioneer Years,* Cassell.

Penrose, H. (1980) *Wings across the World: an Illustrated History of British Airways,* Cassell.

Robertson, B. (1969) *British Military Aircraft Serials 1912–1969,* Ian Allan.

Roskill, S. W. (1969) *The Navy Air Service, Vol. 1 1908–1918,* Navy Records Society.

Samson, C. R. (1930) *Fights and Flights,* Ernest Benn.

Springs, E. W. (ed) (1927) *War Birds – Diary of an Unknown Aviator,* New York.

Stroud, J. (1962) *Annals of British and Commonwealth Air Transport 1919–1960,* Putnam.

Sturtivant, R. and Page, G. (1992) *Royal Naval Aircraft Serials and Units 1911–919,* Air-Britain (Historians) Ltd.

Travers, E. (1990) *Cross Country,* Hothersall & Travers.

Turner, C. C. (1927) *The Old Flying Days,* Sampson Low.

Wells, H. G. (1914) *An Englishman looks at the World,* Cassell.

Williams, W. A. (1989) *Against the Odds – The Life of Group Captain Lionel Rees,* VC, Bridger Books.

Appendix 1

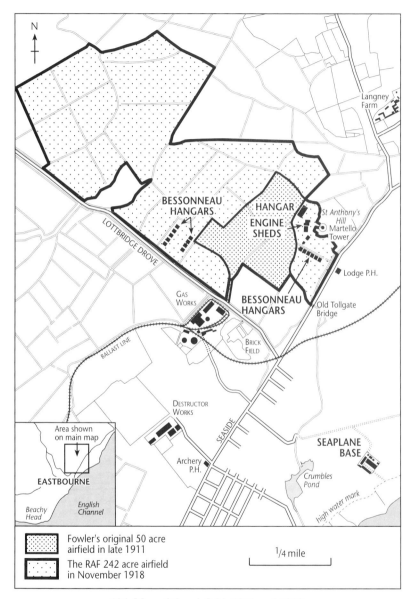

N

Langney Farm

BESSONNEAU HANGARS

HANGAR

St Anthony's Hill

ENGINE SHEDS

Martello Tower

LOTTBRIDGE DROVE

Lodge P.H.

GAS WORKS

BESSONNEAU HANGARS

Old Tollgate Bridge

BALLAST LINE

BRICK FIELD

DESTRUCTOR WORKS

SEASIDE

SEAPLANE BASE

Archery P.H.

Crumbles Pond

high water mark

Area shown on main map

EASTBOURNE

Beachy Head

English Channel

Fowler's original 50 acre airfield in late 1911

The RAF 242 acre airfield in November 1918

¹/₄ mile

106. Map of the airfield, 1911 and 1918.

Sources: 1911 map: Goodall, M. H.: Eastbourne Aviation Company 1911–1924: *Air Pictorial,* March 1979.
1918 map: *RAF Survey,* November 1918.

Appendix 2

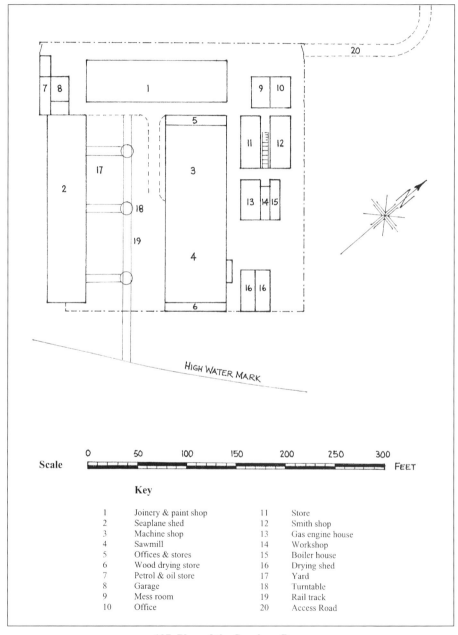

Scale

0   50   100   150   200   250   300   FEET

Key

1	Joinery & paint shop	11	Store
2	Seaplane shed	12	Smith shop
3	Machine shop	13	Gas engine house
4	Sawmill	14	Workshop
5	Offices & stores	15	Boiler house
6	Wood drying store	16	Drying shed
7	Petrol & oil store	17	Yard
8	Garage	18	Turntable
9	Mess room	19	Rail track
10	Office	20	Access Road

107. Plan of the Seaplane Base.

Appendix 3

Aircraft constructed by Eastbourne Aviation Company

Type	Engine	Quantity	Works No	Contract	Serial	Delivered
1912 Monoplane?*		1				
1912 Blériot type	50 hp Gnome	1†				
1913 Biplane	35 hp Anzani	1				
1913 Monoplane	35 hp Anzani	1				
Lt Hunt's Biplane	50 hp Gnome	1				
Military Biplane	80 hp Gnome	1	36			
Circuit Seaplane	100 hp Green	1	37			
BE2c	75 hp Renault	6			1183–1188	July–Nov 1915
BE2c	90 hp RAF	6	118–123	CP63855/15	8404–8409	July–Oct 1916
M Farman S11	80 hp Renault	20	124–143	CP114966/16	N5060–5079	Dec 1916–June 1917
M Farman S11	80 hp Renault	20	144–163	CP103698/17	N6310–6329	July–Nov 1917
Avro 504A	80 hp Gnome	50	201–250	AS18919	D1601–1650	Jan–May 1918
Avro 504K		50	324–373	35A/191/C80	E4324–4373‡	
Avro 504K§		50			F9696–9745	
Avro 504K		50			H5240–5289	
Avro 504L Seaplane	130 hp Clerget	6	E1–E6			

* *Air Pictorial* of March 1979 refers to a 'new type monoplane' built in the spring of 1912.
† There may have been three Blériot types built at EAC (*Eastbourne Gazette,* 11 December 1912).
‡ E4332 was flown by 206 TDS, Eastbourne, as a 504J (13 July 1918).
§ May have been built by Hewlett & Blondeau Ltd (per Robertson, B.: *British Military Aircraft Serials 1912–1969* and Jackson, A. J.: *Avro Aircraft since 1908*).

Appendix 4

The EAC Monoplane

This single-seater tractor monoplane, designed by Emil Gassler, was built during 1913. It used a three-cylinder 35 hp Anzani radial engine driving a 7 ft diameter Rapid propeller and was mounted on the nose of a rectangular section fuselage, metal-covered as far back as the rear of the cockpit and tapered from a deep belly beneath the cockpit to a knife-edge at the tail.

The machine, which was described and illustrated at length in Flight of 3 May 1913, incorporated a one-piece elevator operating below a cut-out in the rudder which was braced by a strut to the top of the fuselage. The wings were mounted just below the upper longerons and employed interconnected ailerons instead of the more usual wing warping, so eliminating twisting strains and giving improved flying characteristics. Flying wires were connected to an under-fuselage pylon while landing loads were taken by wires attached to a single A-shaped pylon in front of the cockpit. The undercarriage axle was sprung by means of rubber shock absorbers.

The design of the EAC monoplane owed something to the Dyott monoplane, which was completed early in 1913 and which enjoyed a series of successful exhibition flights in the USA during 1913. In November 1913, while taking part in a London–Brighton handicap, the Dyott was forced to land on Beachy Head and was blown over onto its back.

Only one EAC Monoplane was built.

Dimensions: Span 29 ft 2 in; Length: 21 ft; Wing area: 135 sq ft.

Performance: Cruising speed 50 mph.

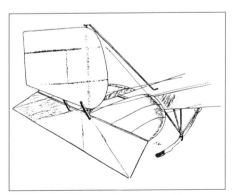

108. Empennage and tail skid.

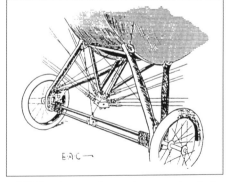

109. Vee-type undercarriage constructed of wood.

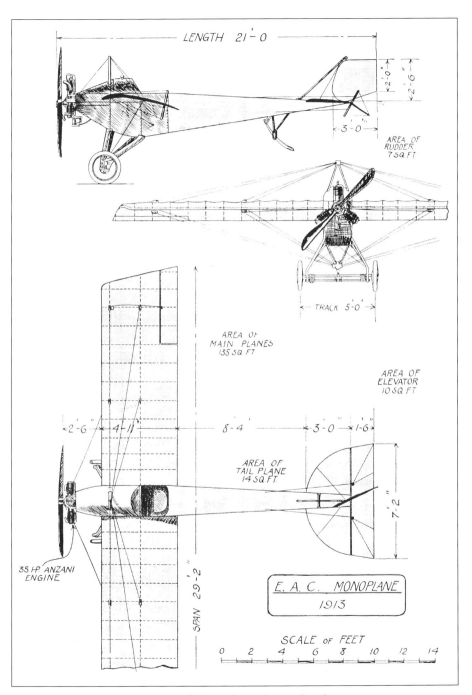

110. The EAC Monoplane – layout drawings.

Appendix 5

RAeC Certificates gained at Eastbourne prior to the war

Cert No	Name	Aircraft	Date
175	F. B. Fowler	EAC Blériot	16 Jan 1912
306	Victor Yates	EAC Blériot	1 Oct 1912
320	Lt R. G. H. Murray	EAC Bristol	15 Oct 1912
349	Cyril E. Foggin	EAC Blériot	29 Oct 1912
350	Emil L. Gassler	EAC Blériot	29 Oct 1912
359	Frank W. Lerwill	EAC Bristol	12 Nov 1912
398	Lt A. C. G. Brown, RN	EAC Bristol	21 Jan 1913
419	F. F. R. Minchin	EAC Bristol	18 Feb 1913
452	A. A. B. Thomson	EAC Bristol	1 April 1913
474	Sub-Lt T. A. Rainey, RNR	EAC Bristol	2 May 1913
535	2nd Lt R. F. Morkill	EAC Biplane†	1 July 1913
558	W. S. Roberts	EAC Bristol	3 July 1913
578	S. J. V. Fill	EAC Biplane†	3 Aug 1913
619	2nd Lt L. Playfair	EAC Biplane†	11 Sept 1913
627	Lt R. J. Bone, RN	EAC Biplane*†	16 Aug 1913
629	F. G. Bevis	EAC Biplane†	13 Sept 1913
664	Lt C. H. Oxlade, RNR	EAC Biplane†	25 Oct 1913
715	Lt R. E. B. Hunt	EAC Biplane†	22 Dec 1913
829	D. Gwynne	EAC Biplane†	30 June 1914
831	J. E. B. Thornely	EAC Biplane†	5 July 1914

*According to Bone's own account (see p. 47), he qualified on a Bristol Biplane.

†According to RAF Museum records, these men qualified on an EAC Biplane.
 As the 1912 photograph confirms, there was an EAC-built biplane at the airfield at this time.

Appendix 6

Lieutenant Hunt's Biplane

This aeroplane, built for exhibition flying to the order of Mr R. E. B. Hunt, was completed in February 1914, a mere two months after Hunt achieved his Certificate. It was a single-seater tractor biplane, fitted with a 50 hp Gnome engine, and designed by Mr Gassler. Unfortunately, no layout drawings exist for the machine, which was reported to have a cruising speed of 65 mph. *Flight* featured the machine on 7 March 1914. Hunt was reported to have taken the machine with him when he joined the Royal Flying Corps later in 1914.

111. Gassler and Hunt with Hunt's biplane.

Appendix 7

The EAC Military Biplane

This aeroplane, extensively reviewed in *Flight* on 21 March and 18 April 1914, was evidence of Fowler's ambition to enter the military market. Designed by Gassler, it was exhibited at the 1914 Olympia Aero Show in March and commented favourably upon by HM King George V.

The aircraft was a tandem two-seater tractor biplane with a rather long square-section fuselage carrying an 80 hp Gnome engine partly enclosed by an aluminium cowl and driving an 8 ft 6 in diameter propeller. The wings were of unequal length, the lower pair shorter than the upper, while a slight taper was incorporated into the leading edges. To improve visibility for the crew, the lower wing roots and the upper centre section were left open. The undercarriage incorporated short forward projecting skids and was sprung by means of rubber cords.

Special features included robust construction combined with light weight, ease of erection and dismantling and, unusually, a starting handle in front of the pilot, making it possible to start the engine without swinging the propeller, so enabling the machine to be restarted without outside assistance in the event of forced landings.

No sales resulted and only one was built.

Dimensions: Span 34 ft 6 in; Length 25 ft; Wing area 245 sq ft.

Weight empty: 950 lb.

Performance: Maximum speed 75 mph; Landing speed 50 mph.

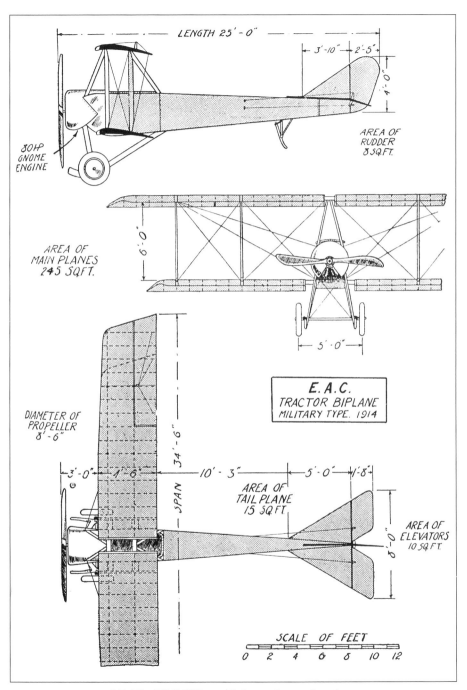

112. The EAC Military Biplane – layout drawings.

137

The EAC Military Biplane – construction details

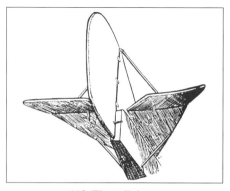

113. The tailplane.

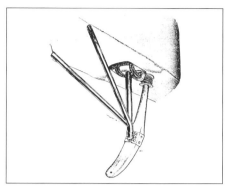

114. The tail skid.

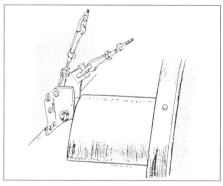

115. Attachment of lower spar to the fuselage. Note the streamline casing round the spar where the wing has been left uncovered.

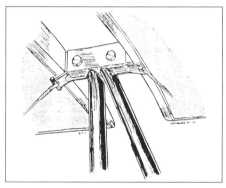

116. Joining the struts and cross members to the fuselage longeron.

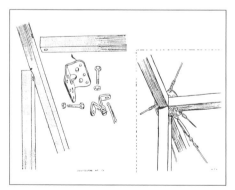

117. Mounting the upper main plane on the cabane.

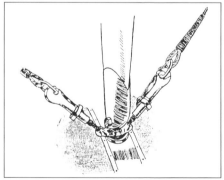

118. Attachment of plane strut and quick-release devices.

Appendix 8

The EAC Circuit Seaplane

This large machine was designed and built as an entrant in the *Daily Mail* 1914 Circuit of Britain Seaplane contest, to be flown by Fowler, and was sponsored by Fowler and Frank Hucks. The aircraft was accorded a substantial write-up in *Flight* on 4 September and 11 December of that year.

The ambitious design embodied a 100 hp Green engine mounted inside the fuselage driving a pair of 8 ft 6 ins tractor propellers through inclined shafts and bevel gearing. There was a two-seat side-by-side cockpit in the nose of the fuselage. The wings were of conventional parallel form with the trailing edges slightly longer than the leading and large ailerons incorporated in the wing tips.

The aeroplane was supported in the water by a pair of floats set 12 ft apart; these, at 19 ft. in length, were judged long enough to avoid the need for wing or tail floats. They also incorporated a novel feature in the form of two welded pipes running from front to rear whose object was to break the partial vacuum which tended to prevent such machines from leaving the surface.

The principle of transmitting the drive through two inclined shafts was attractive, but less than satisfactory in practice because of the tendency of the struts to distort when full power was applied. There is no evidence of the aircraft undergoing trials and it was in fact being modifed when war broke out and the contest for which it was designed was cancelled. It was later broken up.

119. The EAC Circuit Seaplane showing the air tubes between the front of the float and the steps.

Dimensions: Span 54 ft;
　　　　　　　Length 31 ft;
　　　　　　　Wing area 700 sq ft.

Weight: Empty 1,850 lb; Loaded 2,809 lb.

Fuel Capacity: Petrol 70 gal; Oil 6 gal.

Endurance: 7 hours.

Performance: Maximum speed 65 mph; Landing speed 45 mph.

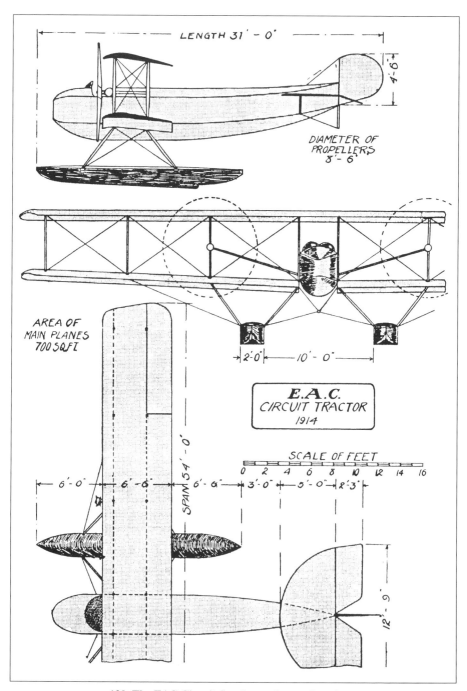

120. The EAC Circuit Seaplane – layout drawings.

Appendix 9

Orders, Awards and Decorations, as awarded between 1914 and 1919.

Victoria Cross (VC) is awarded, per the amended Royal Warrant of August 1858, to officers and men 'for acts of conspicuous courage and bravery under circumstances of extreme danger'.

Companion of the Most Honourable Order of the Bath (CB) is awarded to selected senior officers for services in action (also to civilians for political services).

Commander of the Most Excellent Order of the British Empire (CBE) is awarded to officers of the fighting services for services of a non-combatant character. From December 1918, it was awarded 'for services in the field or before the enemy which do not qualify them for some other order or decoration'.

Distinguished Service Order (DSO) is awarded 'for officers who have rendered distinguished service under fire or under conditions equivalent to service in actual combat with the enemy'.

Officer of the Most Excellent Order of the British Empire (OBE) is a junior grade of the order (see CBE above).

Distinguished Service Cross (DSC) is awarded to naval officers below the rank of Lieutenant Commander 'in recognition of meritorious or distinguished service which may not be sufficient to warrant the appointment of such officers to the DSO'.

Military Cross (MC) is awarded 'to commissioned officers of Captain and below and warrant officers for distinguished and meritorious service in time of war'.

Distinguished Flying Cross (DFC) is awarded to officers and warrant officers of the Air Forces for 'an act or acts of valour, courage, or devotion to duty performed while flying in active operations against the enemy'.

Air Force Cross (AFC) is granted to officers and warrant officers of the Air Forces 'for an act or acts of valour, courage or devotion to duty whilst flying, though not in active operations against the enemy'.

Mention in Dispatches (MiD) was first used in May 1843 to bring the services of deserving officers (and later men) to the attention of higher authority.

Croix de Guerre is a French award given to all ranks of the armed services and citizens of France, also personnel of the Allied Forces, who have been individually mentioned in dispatches.

Appendix 10

Commanding Officers – RNAS/RAF Eastbourne

5 August 1914 to 18 March 1915*	Frederick Bernard Fowler, as a civilian until 1 February 1915, when he was appointed Flight Lieutenant (T) RNAS.
18 March 1915* to 18 March 1916*	Squadron Commander Philip Alfred Shepherd.
18 June 1916* to 18 September 1916*	Squadron Commander Charles Edward Henry Rathbone (former Captain, Royal Marines).
9 November 1916 to 1 May 1917*	Station closed (Sub-Lieutenant R. Spickernell RNVR in command).
13 April 1917 to 31 October 1917	Squadron Commander Cuthbert M. Murphy.
31 October 1917 to 18 March 1918*	Squadron Commander (T) Frederick Bernard Fowler.
18 March 1918*	Lieutenants R. Spickernell and A. E. Taylor.
May 1918 to November 1918† (and possibly later)	Major Henry S. Lees-Smith, RAF (on transfer from the South African Defence Force).

*Dates shown thus are taken from the Navy Lists which are published quarterly and are therefore approximate. Other dates are taken from the officers' service records at the PRO.

†These dates have been estimated. Major Lees-Smith had been wounded while flying in France in 1917 and 1918. Sometime in 1918–1919, he was lodging at 5 Seaville Drive, St Anthony's Hill, Eastbourne, near to the entrance to the airfield.

Note: On the creation of the Royal Air Force on 1 April 1918, RNAS Eastbourne became for a short while 206 Training Depot Station (TDS). The RAF transferred 54 TS from Castle Bromwich to Eastbourne to form the nucleus of 50 TDS on 6 July 1918, aircraft types being standardised as Avro 504K, DH9 and DH9A. The Station was re-designated as 50 TDS on 15 July 1918.

Sources: Ashworth, C. (1990): *Action Stations 9: Military Airfields of the Central South and South East.*
Sturtivant, R.: British Flying Training in World War One, *Cross and Cockade International,* Vol 25, No 1 (1994).

Appendix 11

Relative Ranks

Royal Navy	Royal Flying Corps 1912–18 Royal Air Force 1918–19 Army	Royal Naval Air Service 1912–18	Royal Air Force 1919–Present
Commodore	Brigadier		Air Commodore
Captain	Colonel	Wing Captain	Group Captain
Commander	Lieutenant Colonel	Wing Commander	Wing Commander
Lieutenant Commander	Major	Squadron Commander (when in command)	Squadron Leader
Lieutenant, of over 4 years seniority (Senior to all Flight Commanders).	Captain	Squadron Commander (not in command)	Flight Lieutenant
Lieutenant, of over 4 years seniority	Captain	Flight Commander	Flight Lieutenant
Lieutenant	Captain	Flight Lieutenant	Flight Lieutenant
Sub-Lieutenant	Lieutenant	Flight Sub-Lieutenant	Flying Officer
Midshipman	Second Lieutenant		Pilot Officer

Sources: Mottram, G.: The Early Days of the RNAS, *Cross and Cockade Great Britain,* Vol 10, No 3 (1979). Fowler, S., Elliott, P., Nesbit, R. C. and Goulter, C.: *RAF Records in the PRO.*

Appendix 12

A limited chronology of Fowler's war service

1.2.15	Joins RNAS, appointed Flight Lieutenant (T)*
29.3.15	Isle of Grain – crashed in Short 74 seaplane (74) when an aileron jammed‡
26.5.15	Isle of Grain – Anti-Zeppelin patrol (2328–0005) in Short 830 (1337)†
7.6.15	Eastchurch – Hostile aircraft patrol in Avro 504B (1012)‡
1.8.15	Rainham – Hostile aircraft patrol in Bristol Scout C (1260)‡
9.8.15	Isle of Grain – Hostile aircraft patrol (0349–0635) in Short 184 (844)†
7.10.15	Eastchurch – testing tail guide trestle strop – Bristol Scout (1246)‡
3.11.15	Eastchurch – flight from deck of *Vindex* – Bristol Scout (1255)‡
4.12.15	Posted to Central Flying School, Upavon*
24.1.16	Posted to Isle of Grain*
9.2.16	Isle of Grain – Hostile aircraft patrol (1620–1720) in FBA flying boat (3201)†
20.2.16	Isle of Grain – Hostile aircraft patrol (1138–1240) in FBA flying boat (3201)†
	Eastchurch – Hostile aircraft patrol in Bristol Scout (3015)
19.3.16	Isle of Grain – Hostile aircraft patrol (1500–1545) in FBA flying boat (3206)†
5.5.16	Posted to RNAS Cranwell* (HMS *Daedalus*) as Senior Instructor.
30.6.16	Promoted Flight Commander (T)*
23.4.17	Posted to RNAS Eastbourne*
30.6.17	Promoted Squadron Commander (T)*
31.10.17	Appointed Commanding Officer, RNAS, Eastbourne*
17.5.18	Posted to School of Aeronautics*
21.7.18	Posted to Armaments School*
24.8.18	Posted to Stockbridge*
29.11.18	Posted to 43 TDS (Chattis Hill, near Stockbridge, Hants) from 3 TDS (Lopcombe Corner, near Andover, Hants)*
10.1.19	Posted to Wimbledon*
10.2.19	Transferred to the unemployed list

* PRO Records
† Cole and Cheeseman
‡ Sturtivant and Page

Fowler is reputed to have served also at Dunkirk, Hamble and Stonehenge. In all, he flew some 2,000 hours; the flights and postings listed above are those that have been documented.

Appendix 13

RNAS pupils gaining Certificates at Eastbourne

Cert No	Name	Aircraft	Date
936	Vincent Nicholl	EAC Biplane	8 Oct 1914
937	Francis Gilmer Tempest Dawson	EAC Biplane	8 Oct 1914
938	Maurice Edward Arthur Wright	EAC Biplane	8 Oct 1914
942	John Joseph Petre	EAC Biplane	14 Oct 1914
962	Bertrand Lawrence Huskisson	EAC Biplane	28 Oct 1914
970	Douglas Iron	EAC Biplane	28 Oct 1914
1165	Colin Johnson	Bristol Biplane	11 April 1915
1166	Cyril Tollemache	Bristol Biplane	11 April 1915
1174	George Turner Cain	Bristol Biplane	15 April 1915
1186	Reginald Marsh Everett	Bristol Biplane	21 April 1915
1220	Frank Fowler	Bristol Biplane	30 April 1915
1232	Frank Hartley Aspden	Bristol Biplane	11 May 1915
1325	Lionel Arthur Hervey	Short Biplane	1 June 1915
1359	Arthur Hugh Sandwell	Caudron Biplane	16 June 1915
1366	William Arthur Dalzell	Caudron Biplane	2 June 1915
1368	John Clifford Croft	Caudron Biplane	10 June 1915
1384	Taunton Elliott Viney	Caudron Biplane	1 July 1915
1386	Samuel Denys Felkin	Caudron Biplane	3 July 1915
1393	Henry Seymour Neville	Caudron Biplane	1 July 1915
1402	Eric Lawford Trower	Caudron Biplane	18 June 1915
1407	Henry Carslake Thorold	Caudron Biplane	3 July 1915
1489	Charles Adrian Maitland Heriot	M. Farman Biplane	31 July 1915
1500	Charles Hamilton Murray Chapman	M. Farman Biplane	31 July 1915
1531	Louis Clement Keeble	Caudron Biplane	29 July 1915
1607	John Bevan Cussen	M. Farman Biplane	5 Aug 1915
1632	George Shanks	Caudron Biplane	12 Aug 1915
1649	Frederick Esk Sandford	M. Farman Biplane	5 Aug 1915
1653	William Croucher	M. Farman Biplane	20 Aug 1915
1674	Henry Guy Rivers Malet	Caudron Biplane	30 July 1915
1792	Gerrard William Reginald Fane	M. Farman Biplane	6 Sept 1915
1810	Henry Victor German	Grahame-White Biplane	1 Oct 1915
1820	Arthur Edmond Hawker	M. Farman Biplane	20 Aug 1915
1824	Reginald Rhys Soar	Grahame-White Biplane	1 Oct 1915
1834	Jack Henry Woolf Barnato	M. Farman Biplane	20 Aug 1915
1841	Norman Carter Blanch	Grahame-White Biplane	7 Oct 1915
1848	Bernard Richards Lee	Grahame-White Biplane	9 Oct 1915
1878	Henry Vernon Worrall	Grahame-White Biplane	30 Sept 1915

1879	John Henry Duncan Montgomery Campbell	Grahame-White Biplane	30 Sept 1915
1880	Sidney Arthur Black	Grahame-White Biplane	11 Oct 1915
1964	Cecil Richard Blagrove	Grahame-White Biplane	9 Oct 1915
1973	Ralph Spickernell	M. Farman Biplane	29 Oct 1915
2050	Harold Percy Watson	Grahame-White Biplane	27 Oct 1915
2051	Henry Alexander James Wilson	Grahame-White Biplane	27 Oct 1915
2055	Eliot Millar King	Grahame-White Biplane	3 Nov 1915
2088	Dennis Gurney Broad	M. Farman Biplane	30 July 1915
2110	Alan Harper Curtis	Grahame-White Biplane	7 Nov 1915
2112	George Horsley Porter	Grahame-White Biplane	25 Nov 1915
2119	Alexander James Long	Grahame- White Biplane	17 Nov 1915
2121	Erith Walter Carlton Williams	Grahame-White Biplane	24 Nov 1915
2129	James Sidney Bolas	Grahame-White Biplane	15 Oct 1915
2131	Llewellyn Edwards	Grahame White Biplane	15 Nov 1915
2136	Gerald Arthur MacLean	Grahame-White Biplane	17 Nov 1915
2370	Benjamin Nelson Harrop	M. Farman Biplane	16 Jan 1916
2380	Alfred Irving Hutty	M. Farman Biplane	1 Feb 1916
2409	John James Leslie Patterson	Grahame-White Biplane	21 Nov 1915
2410	Rhys Davies	Grahame-White Biplane	13 Dec 1915
2526	Mervyn Joshua Marshall Bryan	Grahame-White Biplane	20 Sept 1915
2529	Lionel Connor Waite Trend	Grahame-White Biplane	10 Feb 1916
2555	Gilbert Henry Millar	M. Farman Biplane	15 Mar 1916
2556	Herbert Gardner Travers	M. Farman Biplane	23 Jan 1916
2581	Cyril Hargreaves Farquarson Bartholomew	Grahame-White Biplane	5 Dec 1915
2653	Alexander McNeil Proctor	Short Biplane	3 April 1916
2679	James Douglas Scott	BE2c	14 Jan 1916
2709	Thomas Roy Holden	Short Biplane	8 Jan 1916
2715	James Garnet Scott	M. Farman Biplane	7 April 1916
2746	Harold Dent Smith	M. Farman Biplane	16 April 1916
2750	Harry Redmond Wambolt	Short Biplane	8 Jan 1916
2716	Hugh Douglas Macintosh Wallace	M. Farman Biplane	7 April 1916
2806	Dudley Reginald Baylis	M. Farman Biplane	28 April 1916
3152	Oscar Raymond Griffin	Curtiss Biplane	29 June 1916
3197	Robert Alexander Campbell	M. Farman Biplane	27 April 1916
3201	George Denison Kirkpatrick	Curtiss Biplane	19 June 1916
3285	Philip Kenning Fowler	Curtiss Biplane	26 July 1916
3331	Clive Stewart Iron	M. Farman Biplane	24 July 1916
3398	Adam Gil Blakeston Ellis	M. Farman Biplane	17 Aug 1916
3402	Joseph Hubert Solomon	M. Farman Biplane	18 Aug 1916
3422	Eric Stennett Arnold	M. Farman Biplane	18 Aug 1916
3433	Gerald Meyrick Part	M. Farman Biplane	24 Aug 1916

3439	Charles Raymond Walker Hodges	M. Farman Biplane	18 Aug 1916
3462	James Percy White	Curtiss Biplane	21 June 1916
3468	Neville Wall Frames	Curtiss Biplane	12 Aug 1916
3534	Lea Ewart Barnes Wimbush	M. Farman Biplane	23 Aug 1916
3543	Edward Duncan Crundall	M. Farman Biplane	5 Sept 1916
3577	Ronald Beckett Morrison	M. Farman Biplane	10 Aug 1916
3621	Alfred Herbert Stanton Lawson	Curtiss Biplane	21 June 1916
3655	Alfred Cotterill Kermode	M. Farman Biplane	11 Aug 1916
3657	Harcourt Walter Found	M. Farman Biplane	5 Sept 1916
3690	Denis Laird Wilson	M. Farman Biplane	7 Aug 1916
3713	Peter Henry Martin	M. Farman Biplane	8 Sept 1916
3734	Charles Roger Lupton	M. Farman Biplane	14 Sept 1916
3758	Henry Graeme Anderson, MB. FRCS	M. Farman Biplane	26 Oct 1916
3761	Maurice William Buckley	M. Farman Biplane	17 Aug 1916
3771	Gordon Caulfield Wilson Dingwall	M. Farman Biplane	26 May 1916
4160	Edward Errol Maitland Heriot	Avro Biplane	2 Aug 1916
4704	William Knox Denham	M. Farman Biplane	4 June 1916
4716	Donald Alexander Haig	M. Farman Biplane	17 May 1917
4789	Denis Holcombe Carey	M. Farman Biplane	10 May 1917
4900	John Percival White		7 June 1917
4903	John Whiddon Courtenay Reynell	M. Farman Biplane	9 June 1917
4904	Vernon Francis Symondson	M. Farman Biplane	12 June 1917
4962	William Frederick Victor Stephenson	Avro Biplane	11 July 1917
5005	Hugh Wilfrid Reid	M. Farman Biplane	30 May 1917
5006	Henry Scott Ritchie	M. Farman Biplane	10 June 1917
5011	Unsworth Nathaniel Jones	Avro Biplane	17 June 1917
5040	Walter Stanley Magrath	M. Farman Biplane	6 June 1917
5173	Charles Harold Cooper	M. Farman Biplane	2 Sept 1917
5188	Harry Robert Mayes	M. Farman Biplane	23 July 1917
5198	Alfred Dunstan Edmund Selby Ades	M. Farman Biplane	2 Sept 1917
5234	Frederick James Noble Jones	M. Farman Biplane	21 Aug 1917
5260	Stephen Charles Strafford	M. Farman Biplane	10 Sept 1917
5360	George Albert Pitt	M. Farman Biplane	4 Sept 1917
5403	Herbert Frank Shaw Kilby	M. Farman Biplane	21 Aug 1917
5532	Gerald Paterson	M. Farman Biplane	22 June 1917
5553	Harold Wesley Yates	M. Farman Biplane	23 May 1917
5604	Frederick Young Banton	*	31 Jan 1918
5747	John Scott Grosvenor	Avro Biplane	22 Jan 1918
6686	George Hamilton Baker	*	21 Oct 1918

*Not recorded in RAF Museum records.

Appendix 14

Herbert Gardner Travers' Eastbourne Diary
(Printed by kind permission of Miss Eva Travers.)

3rd January 1916: letter to his mother:

Royal Naval Air Station, Trinity Place, Eastbourne. . . .

'The wind has been fresh today: too fresh. This afternoon we had a run with some basset hounds for exercise. . . . I am afraid the postage on the two lots of gear will come to a good lot but it is better than buying the stuff again down here. . . .'

The first entry in his first log book was on 5th January 1916: 'Wind direction and velocity: W5. Machine type and number: Maurice Farman 3002[1]. Pilot: [Warrant Officer H. J.] Lloyd. Time in air: Minutes 9. Height: 300/400 ft. Course: Two circuits Eastbourne Aerodrome and two landings. Remarks: Accompanied Mr Lloyd as passenger. Hands placed lightly on controls. Bumpy'.

The first nine minutes were from 11.12 to 11.21. He flew again on the afternoon of the same day and with the same pilot, but this time they were at 2,000 ft and their course was north from the aerodrome past Polegate and return. His remarks: 'Accompanied Mr Lloyd as passenger. Took no part whatever in controls. Machine very steady above 800'.

On 8 January he did some circuits on the same machine but this time the pilot was Hackman. On 9 January, with the wind at NW1, he flew with [Flt Sub-Lieutenant T. R.] Hackman and then Lloyd for a total of six circuits on Maurice Farman 3001[1]. His total flying time for the week ending 9 January was 57 minutes. On 10 January, with the wind at NW4, he flew again with Lloyd on Maurice Farman 3001: 'Course: 3 circuits aerodrome and 3 landings. Remarks: Instruction; had control of machine 2nd and 3rd circuits and landings'.

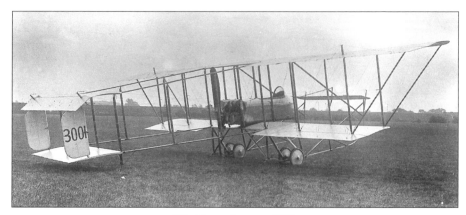

121. Henry Farman 3001.

148

He wrote to Jay [his sister] on 11 January:

'Please thank Dad for his letter which arrived here this evening. We have had some grand weather in patches and my total time up so far has been 1 hr 23 mins.

Today there was nothing doing so six of us went to the rifle range. [The rifle range was on the Crumbles, some few hundred yards from the aerodrome.] I shot with an automatic pistol for the first time. They are very pretty weapons. After that we had some rifle practice at 200. . . . We have plenty of pupils (about 28) of all sorts here, most of them are rattling good fellows. The Canadians are very keen. . . . The C.O. [probably Squadron Commander Rathbone] is a live man. I am very lucky to be under a decent (sub) acting flight commander. Both he and the WO who does most of the instruction are sound, good, pilots. The WO Mr Lloyd makes most perfect landings.

As you know I am being taught on a "mechanical cow" (MF).

Today on the range Lloyd and I tied top so we shot it off with 5 rounds. . . .'

He flew again on 14 January, with the wind at NNW3, on M[aurice] Farman 3002 with Lloyd, one flight of 13 minutes, the next of four minutes. And again on 16 January, with the wind at NW2, for ten minutes at 300 ft and made two landings. Later the same morning on the same machine, 3002, he flew again with Lloyd, this time for seven minutes at 300/400 ft. Later on the same morning he went solo. He flew for ten minutes at 1,000 ft, doing figures of eight round the aerodrome on 3002; he noted in his remarks column: 'made first solo flight landing too fast but no damage done'. He made a further solo flight half an hour later, flying at 600 ft on the same machine. The week closed; his total recorded flying time was 141 minutes of which the last 25 minutes were solo.

One week later he flew again, doing a refresher solo on 3002; later the same morning he had his first passenger flight (with Hackman) on BE2c 1184 [which had been built at EAC], at 300 ft; then at 11.50 the same morning he flew for 28 minutes at 1,600 ft on MF 3002, doing figures of eight round the gasworks and to the NE of the aerodrome. It was his qualifying flight. His remarks record: 'Solo. Ticket Flight. Bumpy up to 800. Very steady 800/1600. Qualified'. He had done 64 minutes solo. Later the same day he flew MF 3001 solo off to have a look at Pevensey Castle. Remarks: 'This machine was lower powered than 3002'. On 26 January, with the wind at W2, he was Lt Newberry's[2] passenger on Curtiss [JN3] 3374 out to the Downs and back. H's remarks: 'Compared MF this machine is nose heavy and quick on lateral control. She also carries stb'd helm'.

He wrote to Emmie [his mother] on 28 January:

'Thanks very much for your postcard. . . . Very little flying since I last wrote. Could you send me my *Aviation, Map-Reading, The Manual of RFC Training*, both parts, Wood's *Strength and Elasticity of Structural Members*. I am afraid this is a big list but if you could include the old report of the aircraft factory too it might be useful. I would come home and fetch them but I do not want to miss any flying (and) not ask for leave as soon as this.

I am afraid you have had a very anxious time lately – don't overwork yourself, Mum, . . . by the way, you were right about turning into or with the wind.'

On 29 January, with the wind at SE1, he again flew with Lt Newberry on Curtiss 3374, receiving instruction and landing on the Downs. Later the same day he flew MF 3001 solo round Beachy Head, Polegate Woods, Willingdon and return. Remarks: 'Thick clouds from 1,000 to 2,000. But very steady above'. Later the same day, with the wind at SW2, he flew MF 3007 solo round Bexhill, making two circuits of the town. Remarks: 'Engine stopped when coming down over Pevensey 2,800 ft. Forced landing. Machine dismantled'.

The week ending 7 February he had no flying.

On 8 February, with the wind at W5, he flew MF 3002 near the aerodrome at 1,950 ft. Remarks: 'Wind coming over Beachy Head gusty and bumpy. Landing over corner big shed. Too much engine and too fast. n.d.d'.

On 9 February he was out again on the Curtiss 3374 with Lt Newberry; they landed near Wilmington three times; later the same day, with the wind at N3, he went solo on Curtiss 3392, keeping near the aerodrome. Remarks: 'first solo on a Curtiss machine: climbs slowly at first. 1½ S turns to land'. In the afternoon of the same day, with the wind at NW2, he flew the same machine at 2,500 ft. Remarks: 'This machine with a 4-bladed prop. climbs slowly at first; S turns (3) to land'.

Later the same day he flew Curtiss 3374 to 2,000 ft, with the wind at NW3, for 26 minutes. Remarks: '(2-bladed prop) climbs well. Engine started missing badly – would not climb above this height. Left wing apt to drop'. On 12 February Lt Newberry took him up for a short flight on Bristol [TB8] 1224 near the aerodrome. Remarks: '1st passenger flight on Bristol'. On the afternoon of the same day, with the wind at NNW2, he went solo on the same machine for 26 minutes, flying at 4,300 ft over Beachy Head. Remarks: '1st solo on Bristol. Perfect day. 1st experience of Gnome engine. Climb 45 level 54'. Later on the same afternoon Lt McMinnies[3] took him up on BE2c 1187 [built at EAC] for 22 minutes, practising bomb dropping over Langney Point and target N. of

122. Bristol TB8 1224.

field. On 19 February Lt Jamieson took him up for 51 minutes on BE2c 1184, with the wind at NW6. They flew NW from the aerodrome to Hailsham then west to Lewes and return. Remarks: 'Used this flight for observation practice. Wind very bumpy near ground. Steady about 3,000'.

On 20 February, with the wind at SE2, he flew Bristol [TB8] 1224 for 31 minutes at 3,600 ft near the aerodrome. Remarks: 'Rain, hail and snow at 3,600 and all the way down to 900. Could not see. Came in'. But he took off again on the same machine about an hour later, at noon, and climbed to 4,100 ft near the aerodrome and Beachy Head. Remarks: 'When between Beachy Head and town ran out of petrol. Landed in field near aerodrome, filled up and returned. At 3.20 on the same afternoon he took the same machine up to 5,150 ft for 40 minutes over Beachy Head. Remarks: 'Small clouds at 4,500 ft. 5,150 highest yet reached. Weather perfect. Cold'.

He did some more practice landings on the same machine during the remainder of the afternoon and on the following morning, with the wind at ESE5: 'Was up again on Bristol 1224, climbing to 5,100 over Beachy Head Road. Spotting gunfire. Getting more confidence. Wind steady'. He did some more practice landings and then went up again with Scott as pilot over the aerodrome. Remarks: 'Was to spot gunfire but snowstorm sent us down'.

He was at Eastchurch for one day, 25 February, although still stationed at Eastbourne. His log book records: 'Wind NE3. Bristol [TB8] 1218. 6 minutes. 800 ft. Round Eastchurch (Isle of Sheppey). Remarks: Testing strange machine. Bad get off. Good landing'. He had probably been sent to Eastchurch in order to find his way back to Eastbourne, for on the next day he returned to his own station.

'26/2/16. Wind ESE4. Bristol Tractor 1218A. 88 minutes. 2,900 ft. From Eastchurch 215°. Passed Headcorn and Robertsbridge. To Eastbourne. Remarks: 1st long cross country. Steered a compass course and checked by ma/c passing. Snow on ground and 3 snowstorms in the air prevented machine from going higher. Lost 300 ft in one snowstorm. Engine started 1,075 revs afterwards dropped to 1,050.'

Back at Eastbourne, he made a number of further flights on Bristol Tractor A 1218 around the aerodrome, testing the engine, cleaning the petrol supply; he really does not seem to have liked the machine at all. On 1 March he remarked: 'Experimenting with needle valve. Cut down petrol too much. Came into aerodrome too flat'.

Later on the same afternoon he went up with Jamieson as pilot on Blériot [type X1] 3215. The wind was at S2 and they were up for 7 minutes at 180 ft over the aerodrome. Remarks: 'Machine could hardly get away from very heavy ground and climbed slowly. First experience as passenger on monoplane'.

Later the same afternoon, with the wind at SE1, he went solo on Blériot 3214 for eight minutes at 1,000 ft over the aerodrome. Remarks: 'First solo on Blériot. Weather perfect. Found no difficulty in getting off or landing. Made turns of large radius. (Petrol 22, 1,200 revs climbs 45 level 54)'. By now the light had gone but the following morning, 2nd March, with the wind at NE2, he was up again, on Blériot 3236 this time, practising landings. On the afternoon of 2 March he went up with Lloyd as pilot on Maurice Farman 3001, his dear old 'mechanical cow', to do a bit of bomb-dropping practice. Their course was: Pevensey Castle, Herstmonceux Castle, Gardner Street, Dallington Church, Ashburnham House, Battle Abbey, Pevensey Castle, aerodrome. Remarks: 'Bomb-dropping practice. Floods to starboard. Country getting hilly. Fired two *Very's* light. Large woods and lake. The rain clouds were not above 1,000 ft, making observation very difficult'.

On Monday 6 March, with the wind at N5, he was sent out solo to drop a bomb at Dallington. He was on Bristol Tractor A 1218, the machine which he had brought from Eastchurch. 'Course: Compass Co. N. This was wrong because Dallington was objective. When 1 mile due E Hailsham forced landing. Remarks: Set out solo for Dallington to drop one bomb (*Very's* light). Engine doing 1,050 at start, afterwards 1,060. At Hailsham dropped to 1,000 then 950. Came down in good stubble field (Woodland's Farm). 1 spiral and S turn good landing – phoned for assistance. L. M. Young found partial air lock in petrol feed'.

He wrote to Emmie on 13 March:

'Thank you for your letter just arrived. I have been away most of this week.

On Monday I had a forced landing engine trouble about 9 miles away but picked out a good field and flew back in the afternoon. On Tuesday I went out in a car to help another fellow who had had his forced landing about 20 miles away. On Thursday I went over to Shoreham as a passenger to fetch another machine but spent 2 days thawing it up. So went back on Saturday night and flew over again on Sunday and brought it back. I am very fit and hope everyone at home is also. . . . Please thank J. for cuffs. I will write soon. They are very warm and just right. . . .'

He had done a lot of practice on Blériot 3214 and really liked the machine. One of his remarks was: 'These machines are much easier to land without engine than with it. Owing to electric light knife switch being used instead of small press button'.

On 9 March he was flying alone on Curtiss [JN3] 3356 near Shoreham Aerodrome when, at 200 ft: 'Engine cut out completely at 150 feet on edge aerodrome (low tension trouble). Turn back quickly. Engine cut in again. Made good landing. Right wing down in air'.

The following day he tested the machine with a new magneto. 'Very good.'

On 12 March McMinnies took him up on Henry Farman [F22] 1519 for 30 minutes at 3,200 ft near the aerodrome: Remarks: 'First passenger flight on Henry Farman. Visibility good. Weather perfect'. Later the same morning he took up Blériot 3214 near the aerodrome. Remarks: 'Engine ran well on ground but missed in air. Missing became worse so came in'.

In the afternoon he went up in BE2c with McMinnies and they went to Polegate, Lewes and Shoreham. Remarks: 'Engine rev counter came adrift at Polegate. Slightly misty'. On the same afternoon he took up Curtiss 3356 for 61 minutes. This must have been the flight he mentioned to his mother. 'Course: Shoreham to N. Brighton, Lewes, Glynde, Polegate, Eastbourne. Remarks: black clouds drifted up from E and ground was invisible at 2,000 ft. Climbed to 3,000. Comp. Co100°. Came below clouds near Lewes and again took compass course 130°. Very dark low clouds when landing at Eastbourne. Good landing. Climb 50 level 60 K'.

On 15 March he was once again struggling with Bristol 1218, which he took up for 18 minutes to 2,000 ft near Eastbourne Aerodrome. Remarks: 'Testing engine 1,100 revs at first later dropped to 1,080. Cut down petrol from four turns to 1¼ (slowly). Revs dropped to 1,050. Came down and found mag distributor brush crooked. Weather perfect.' He tested 1218's engine again on the 16th. Remarks: 'Testing engine. 1,080 revs steady. Petrol 2 turns'.

Later on, during the morning of 16 March, he went solo on BE2c, flying for 23 minutes and taking the machine up to 3,600 ft near Eastbourne Aerodrome and over Polegate, Elm Town [probably a transcription error for Old Town] and Pevensey. Remarks: 'First solo on BE2c. Hands off controls from 2,000 up. Came down in large circles hands off'.

On 18 March he was once again up on Bristol 1218 for 12 minutes, testing the engine over the aerodrome at 500 ft. Remarks: 'Testing engine 1,080 revs'.

But at 10.35 on the same morning he took Henry Farman 1519 up solo for 28 minutes at 2,500 ft over the aerodrome. Remarks: 'First solo on Henry Farman. Takes left rudder (opposite to tractor Gnomes). Very flyable machine answers controls'. He had landed at 11.03 and an hour later, at 12.04, he took up his first pasenger, Grove, for 41 minutes on Henry Farman 1519; they stayed near the aerodrome, in good weather, observing some live bomb dropping. In the evening of the same day, at 6 o'clock, he went up again on Henry Farman 1519 alone. Remarks: 'Practising turns. Machine very pleasant to handle'.

And there ended his basic flying training at RNAS, Eastbourne, for, by 1 April 1916 (his 25th birthday), he had been transferred to the Gunnery School at Eastchurch.

1. Travers refers to these aircraft as Maurice Farmans. According to Robertson: *British Military Aircraft Serials*, they were Henry Farmans (see illustration on page 148).

2. Flight Lieutenant (later Flight Commander) J. D. Newberry was a South African who was for 18 months an instructor at RNAS, Eastbourne. He later served in France and was awarded the Croix de Guerre. He died in a flying accident in England in September 1917, aged 23.

3. Lieutenant (later Major) William Gordon McMinnies was in civilian life an editor of technical journals. He served as an instructor at Eastbourne, Vendôme, Cranwell and Redcar and was discharged from the RAF in May 1919. While at Eastbourne he lodged at 17 The Avenue.

Appendix 15

Extract from the RAF Survey of 1 November 1918
Eastbourne
No 50 – Training Depot Station (SE Area; No 2 Group, 60th Wing)

Location: England, Sussex, on the north-eastern outskirts of Eastbourne (pop. 52,500). Polegate Aerodrome is 3 miles north-west. Shoreham Aerodrome is 26 miles west.

Railway Station: Eastbourne (LB & SC Rly) 2 miles. There is a railway siding almost to the aerodrome.

Road: The main road, Eastbourne to Pevensey, passes the site.

Function: A Training Depot Station (Three Unit), Single Seater Fighter.

Establishment:

Personnel:		Transport:	
Officers	51	Touring Cars	1
Officers under instruction	120	Light Tenders	10
NCOs under instruction	60	Heavy Tenders	10
WOs and NCOs above the rank		Motor Cycles	8
of Corporal	47	Sidecars	8
Corporals	25	Trailers	5
Rank and File	320		
Forewomen	7		
Women	155		
Women (Household)	54		
	—		—
Total (exclusive of Hostel Staff)	839	Total	42

Machines:	Camel (BR)	36
	Avros	36
	Total	72

Aerodrome: Maximum dimension in yards: 2,000 × 1,000. Area: 242 acres, of which 10 acres are occupied by the Station Buildings, etc. Height above sea-level: 15 ft. Soil: loam on heavy clay. Surface: wet in bad weather and liable to flood. The dykes on the aerodrome are mostly covered by timber bridges, but some of them are uncovered. Level: The general surroundings are low-lying, marshy country. Much cut up by dykes. The town of Eastbourne is close by on the south-west.

Tenure Policy: Not at present on the list of permanent stations.

Accommodation:

Technical Buildings

2 Aeroplane Sheds (179' × 59' and 69' × 69')
MT [Motor Transport] Shed
Tyre Store
4 Workshops: Carpenters 95' × 45', Erecting 20' × 18', Dope 30' × 30', Fabric 30' × 30', Smiths 20' × 15', General 200' × 60'
Oil Stores
2 Petrol Stores
4 General Lecture Huts
Gunnery Workshop
Depot Offices
Flight Offices
Latrines
Compass Platform

Regimental Buildings

Regimental Institute
Regimental Store
2 Men's Huts
5 Men's Dormitories
Men's latrines and Ablution
Reception Station
First Aid Hut
Drying Room
Coal Yard

Note: Officers and other ranks are also accommodated in hired buildings.

State of Works and Buildings: On 1 August 1918, the percentage of progress was as follows:

Sheds: Additional sheds not started	14
Technical Buildings: Workshop and garage in hand.	
Dope Shed: No further progress can be made until completion of garage	50
Regimental Buildings: 5 Dormitories, Bath House, Washing and Drying Room in hand	75
Women's Quarters: nil	—
Roads: Roadwork in hand	30
Water Supply: Extension as necessary	—
Drainage: Satisfactory Progress	64
Sewage	100
Lighting: Extensions as necessary	—
Bridging Dykes and Surface Water Drainage: Work proceeding satisfactorily and nearing completion	98

Appendix 16

Aircraft at RNAS Eastbourne, October 1915

Serial	Type	Engine	Ready
1183	BE2c	70 hp Renault	Yes
3214	Blériot	80 hp Gnome	Yes
3215	Blériot	80 hp Gnome	Yes
3225	Blériot	80 hp Gnome	No
3226	Blériot	80 hp Gnome	Yes
3227	Blériot	80 hp Gnome	No
3236	Blériot	80 hp Gnome	Yes
3237	Blériot	80 hp Gnome	Yes
1224	Bristol TB8	80 hp Gnome	Yes
3265	Caudron GIII	80 hp Gnome	No
3267	Caudron GIII	80 hp Gnome	Yes
3271	Caudron GIII	80 hp Gnome	Yes
3356	Curtiss JN-3	90 hp Curtiss	Yes
3367	Curtiss JN-3	90 hp Curtiss	No
3368	Curtiss JN-3	90 hp Curtiss	Yes
3370	Curtiss JN-3	90 hp Curtiss	No
3371	Curtiss JN-3	90 hp Curtiss	No
3374	Curtiss JN-3	90 hp Curtiss	No
3392	Curtiss JN-3	90 hp Curtiss	Yes
3154	Grahame-White GW XV	60 hp Rhone	No
3157	Grahame-White GW XV	60 hp Rhone	Yes
3160	Grahame-White GW XV	60 hp Rhone	No
1600	Grahame-White 1600	70 hp Gnome	No
1519	Henry Farman F22	80 hp Gnome	Erecting
1599	Henry Farman	80 hp Gnome	Yes
2984*	Maurice Farman S7 Longhorn	70 hp Renault	No
8106	Maurice Farman S11 Shorthorn	70 hp Renault	Yes
8107	Maurice Farman S11 Shorthorn	70 hp Renault	No
8468	Maurice Farman S11 Shorthorn	75 hp Renault	Yes
1173	White & Thompson 'Bognor Bloater'	70 hp Renault	Yes
1175	White & Thompson 'Bognor Bloater'	70 hp Renault	No

* Transferred from military use.

Appendix 17

The Post-War Aircraft Fleet

Avro 504K (built by the Sunbeam Motor Car Co Ltd)

G – EAJG   ex H1956   registered 14.7.19   sold March 1922 (crashed August 1922)

G – EALD   ex H1925   registered 10.6.19   sold May 1922 (serial may be incorrect)

Avro 504L 3-seater (built by EAC)

G – EAFB   ex K144   Works No E1   sold June 1921

G – EASD   E2   sold to Sweden March 1921

G – EASE   E3   for sale June 1921

G – EAJH (seaplane)   E4   sank off Hove 19 August 1920

G – EALO (seaplane)   E5   crashed February 1921

G – EANS   E6   crashed 23 October 1919

Short 184 4-seater Seaplane (built by J. S. White & Co)

G – EALC   ex N2998   registered 17.6.19   scrapped August 1920

G – EAJT   ex N2986*   registered 8.8.19   scrapped August 1920

*Robinson B.: *British Military Aircraft Serials 1912–1969* states that this aircraft is N2968.
A photograph taken off Eastbourne beach clearly shows N2986.

123. Avro 504L Seaplane G-EAFB, built at EAC.

Appendix 18

Ext:- 10.

Broadway Court, Broadway.
Westminster, London. S.W.I.

Please quote:-
Ref:- 193/-

23rd February 1921.

Dear Sir,

It is understood that you are willing to accept an appointment on a special mission proceeding abroad, your contract being for one year. The terms, which it is understood have already been outlined to you, are as follows:-

Salary - £400 per annum.
Free passage to and from destination abroad.
Free outfit.
Free living accommodation, except messing.
Lodging and subsistence allowance whilst away from the Base on duty.

As you no doubt agree with these terms, will you write to that effect.

In any case, proceed to the above address as soon as possible, in order that questions of kit etc. may be arranged for, as you will be required to sale from a British port on the 12th proximo.

I need not impress on you that it is most important to realise that absolute secrecy is highly essential.

Yours faithfully,

COLONEL.

Mr. F. Ford,
    Eastbourne Aviation Co.,
        Eastbourne,
            Sussex.

WS/MAB.

Mission, will formulate regulations as may be required from time to time.

124. Max Ford and his letter of appointment.

Index

For ease of reference, the index is divided into four sections: Aviation, Eastbourne and Environs, People, and Miscellaneous. Most entries are indexed once only.

Aviation